Freedom Is a Constant Struggle

Freedom
Is a
Constant Struggle

**Ferguson, Palestine,
and the Foundations of a Movement**

Angela Y. Davis

Edited by Frank Barat

Haymarket Books
Chicago, Illinois

Published in 2016 by
Haymarket Books
P.O. Box 180165
Chicago, IL 60618
773-583-7884
www.haymarketbooks.org
info@haymarketbooks.org

ISBN: 978-1-60846-564-4

Trade distribution:
In the US, Consortium Book Sales and Distribution, www.cbsd.com
In Canada, Publishers Group Canada, www.pgcbooks.ca
In the UK, Turnaround Publisher Services, www.turnaround-uk.com
All other countries, Publishers Group Worldwide, www.pgw.com

This book was published with the generous support of Lannan Foundation
and Wallace Action Fund.

Cover design by Abby Weintraub.

Special thanks to Karen Domínguez Burke for transcribing the interviews.

Printed in Canada by union labor.

Library of Congress Cataloging-in-Publication data is available.

14

Contents

Foreword

CORNEL WEST

Angela Davis is one of the few great long-distance intellectual freedom fighters in the world. From the revolutionary mass movements of the 1960s to the insurgent social motion in our day, Angela Davis has remained steadfast in her focus on the wretched of the Earth. In stark contrast to most leftists in the academy, her structural analysis and courageous praxis have come at a tremendous cost in her life and for her well-being. As a new assistant professor of philosophy, she was demonized by Governor Ronald Reagan in California. The University of California Board of Regents stripped her of her academic position owing to her membership in the Communist Party. She was put at the top of the FBI's Most Wanted list, on the run from the police forces of the US Empire, and incarcerated after her capture. Her grace and dignity during a historic court trial electrified the world. And her determination to remain true to her revolutionary vocation—in the intense international spotlight—has been an inspiration.

After the systematic state execution or incarceration of Black warriors and government incorporation of Black professionals, Angela

Davis still stands tall with intellectual power and moral fervor. During the thirty-year ice age of neoliberal rule, Angela Davis remained on fire for the freedom of the poor and working people. Her scholarship on women, workers, and people of color helped keep alive a radical vision, analysis, and praxis during the Reagan and Bush years. Her pioneering intellectual and political work on the boomtown growth of the prison system helped set the foundations for the age of Ferguson. And her ubiquitous lecturing, marvelous teaching, and courageous solidarity in every corner of the globe keep candles of hope burning in the cold and chilling days of neoliberal hegemony. She remains—after more than fifty years of struggle, suffering, and service—the most recognizable face of the left in the US Empire.

In this latest text of her magisterial corpus, Angela Davis puts forward her brilliant analyses and resilient witness here and abroad. In a clear and concise manner, she embodies and enacts "intersectionality"—a structural intellectual and political response to the dynamics of violence, white supremacy, patriarchy, state power, capitalist markets, and imperial policies.

On December 3, 2014, I was blessed to stand alongside my dear sister and comrade Angela Davis at the Oxford Union Debate in memory of the fiftieth anniversary of the great Malcolm X's presence at the Oxford Union. It was a grand event—with Angela bringing back the spirit of Malcolm in a magnificent way. This same spirit infuses this book and beckons us to partake of its long-standing joys of serving the people!

Introduction

FRANK BARAT

I am writing this sitting in my small office in Brussels. The month of June is nearly gone and the heat has just arrived.

I work in a building that hosts various organizations and charities working for global justice. Some focus on Western Sahara; some on Palestine; others on torture, Latin America, or Africa. It is a good environment to work in, surrounded by people who believe in a fairer and better society, and who have decided to act on their beliefs and dedicate their lives to trying to change the world. Sounds utopian, maybe. But the important word here is probably not the one you are thinking of. It's *trying*. Trying and trying again. Never stopping. That is a victory in itself. Everyone and everything tells you that "outside" you will not succeed, that it is too late, that we live in an epoch where a revolution cannot happen anymore. Radical changes are a thing of the past. You can be an outsider, but not outside the system, and you can have political beliefs, even radical ones, but they need to stay within the

ANGELA Y. DAVIS

bounds of the permissible, inside that bubble that has been drawn for you by the elites.

My office is located a few steps away from the European Commission headquarters, an imposing building made of grayness and glass that I cycle past every morning. A place that is now flanked by military personnel as well as private security companies. I often wonder what their job is: to protect the people, the human beings inside, or to protect the place itself, the concept, the ideology embodied in it?

This morning, when I visualized Greece in the midst of anti-austerity protests, I saw the contested "Europe." People in the streets, from all walks of life, from various generations, chanting, raising flags, rioting. I saw people organizing. I saw local assemblies, clinics run by volunteers. I saw the Acropolis, Exarchia, Syntagma Square. I saw olive trees. I saw the sun. I saw *dēmokratia*. The rule, the power, of the people. The very concept that has lost most of its meaning in today's world. This is a concept that to the "big guns" of Europe (Germany, France, Italy, the European Central Bank, and the European Commission itself) is only valid and celebrated when it does not diverge from their view of and plans for the world. In the last few months, since the groundbreaking and game-changing elections in Greece, for the first time in Europe a left-wing and anti-austerity party, Syriza, has come into power, and those big guns are trying to make sure that it crumbles and disappears. The party, but more importantly, the message, the idea the party embodies, is under threat. The concept that another way of organizing our lives collectively is possible, that we can be ruled by each other, the 99 percent, instead of technocrats, banks, and corporations. As I write this, the hope that finds expression in the streets and homes all over Greece is a movement. A movement in the midst of a huge loss of material wealth for ordinary Greeks. But there's a message there for everyone and it is that people can unite, that democracy from below can challenge oligarchy, that imprisoned migrants can be freed, that fascism can be overcome, and that equality is emancipatory.

The powerful have sent us a message: obey, and if you seek collective liberation, then you will be collectively punished. In the case of Europe, it's the violence of austerity and borders where migrant lives are negated, allowed to drown in sea buffer zones. In the case of the United States, Black and Native lives are systematically choked by an enduring white supremacy that thrives on oppression and settler colonialism, and is backed by drones, the dispossession of territory and identity to millions, mass incarceration, the un-peopleing of people, and resource grabs that deny that indigenous lives matter and that our planet matters. All around us and up close, we are being told not to care. Not to collectivize, not to confront.

Angela

What can we do? How can we do it? With whom? What tactics should be used? How should we define a strategy that is accessible to everyone, including a general public that has reached levels of de-politicization that can make atrocities seem acceptable? What is our vision? How can we make sure "we" are talking to "everyone"? How can we catalyze and connect sustainable, cross-border, and radical movements? These are the types of questions that many activists ask themselves on a daily basis, questions that are anchored in the present and will shape our future.

It is easy to feel discouraged and simply let go. There is no shame in that. We are, after all, engaged in a struggle that seems, if we look at it using a mainstream political framework and through a mass media prism, unwinnable. On the other hand, if we take a step back, look at things from a broader angle, reflecting on what is happening all over the world and the history of struggle, the history of solidarity movements, it becomes clear, sometimes even obvious, that seemingly indestructible forces can be, thanks to people's willpower, sacrifices, and actions, easily broken.

When I first thought of producing a book with Angela Davis, my main goal was to talk about our struggle as activists. To try to define it in real and concrete terms. To try to understand what it means to people engaged in it. Where and how does it start? Does it ever end? What are the essential foundations for building a movement? What does it mean physically, philosophically, and psychologically?

It was crucial for me to discuss this struggle with Angela because she is, for me and many others, a source of knowledge and inspiration, and we need to learn from her experiences and use the lessons they offer for whatever fight we are involved in. Angela never stopped; she is still, every day, living the struggle. She is an embodiment of resistance and I see her ongoing work and presence reflected in and inspiring to many of the collective liberation movements we see today. It's reflected in the understanding of prison as part of an industrial complex, rooted in slavery and capitalism, and in the popularization of the abolition movement. It's reflected in her support for anticolonial struggles all over the world, including Palestine, where many activists, including me, have taken part in on-the-ground solidarity activism.

The idea of the book was, like the previous ones I edited with Noam Chomsky and Ilan Pappé, to have a flowing conversation and to leave room for some more in-depth essays by Angela that would fill gaps or extend our conversations.

A strong focus of our interviews, with the one in Brussels conducted soon after Ferguson erupted and the one in Paris right after a jury let the police officer who had killed Michael Brown go free, was Palestine and how to build a truly global and social movement around what is today one of the most urgent issues to resolve—an issue that should define where we stand as a movement and as people. The focus was on how to build links with other social struggles. How to explain to people in Ferguson that what is happening in Palestine is also about them, and vice versa for the people of Palestine. How to make the struggle a truly global one, one in which everybody on the planet has a part to play and understands that role. How do we respond collectively to the militarization of our societies? What role can Black feminism play in this process? What does being a prison abolitionist means in concrete terms today?

The interviews addressed these points and more. Some are then developed further in lengthy and powerful essays by Angela, who talks about the struggles for justice in Ferguson and Charleston in particular, and how they go a long way in showing that the struggle for equality and freedom is far from over.

The last two pieces in this book are Angela's reflections on the political struggle from the sixties to the current era of Obama and on transnational solidarity. These are two groundbreaking contributions that should give people tools and arguments to take up the fight and motivate others to become active and join us.

"Angela is a miracle," US author, poet, and activist Alice Walker told me one day. Angela is unique but not exceptional because her example and her work has helped to raise new voices, new scholars, and new activists who take her ideas and expand them. I think when Alice defined Angela as a miracle, she meant that Angela is living proof that it is possible to survive, withstand, and overcome the full force of corporate power and the state fixed on the destruction of one important individual because she inspires collective solidarity. She's living proof that people power works, that an alternative is possible, and that the struggle can be a beautiful and exhilarating one. That is something we need, as human beings, to experience.

And it's in everyone's power to partake in the struggle.

Brussels
June 2015

ONE

Progressive Struggles against Insidious Capitalist Individualism

Interview by Frank Barat (conducted via email over several months in 2014)

You often talk about the power of the collective and stress the importance of the movement, rather than talking about individuals. How can we build such a movement, based on those ethics in a society that promotes selfishness and individualism?

Since the rise of global capitalism and related ideologies associated with neoliberalism, it has become especially important to identify the dangers of individualism. Progressive struggles—whether they are focused on racism, repression, poverty, or other issues—are doomed to fail if they do not also attempt to develop a consciousness of the insidious promotion of capitalist individualism. Even as Nelson Mandela always insisted that his accomplishments were collective, always also achieved by the men and women who were his comrades, the media attempted to sanctify him as a heroic individual. A similar process has attempted to disassociate Dr. Martin Luther King Jr. from the vast numbers of women and men who constituted the very heart of the mid-twentieth-century US freedom movement. It is essential to resist the depiction of history as the work of heroic individuals in order for people today to recognize their potential agency as a part of an ever-expanding community of struggle.

What is left today of the Black Power movement?

I think of the Black Power movement—or what we referred to at the time as the Black liberation movement—as a particular moment in the development of the quest for Black freedom. In many ways it was a response to what were perceived as limitations of the civil rights movement: we not only needed to claim legal rights within the existing society but also to demand substantive rights—in jobs, housing, health care, education, et cetera—and to challenge the very structure of society. Such demands—also against racist imprisonment, police violence, and capitalist exploitation—were summed up in the Ten-Point Program of the Black Panther Party (BPP).

Although Black individuals have entered economic, social, and political hierarchies (the most dramatic example being the 2008 election of Barack Obama), the overwhelming number of Black people are subject to economic, educational, and carceral racism to a far greater extent than during the pre–civil rights era. In many ways, the demands of the BPP's Ten-Point Program are just as relevant—or perhaps even more relevant—as during the 1960s, when they were first formulated.

The election of Barack Obama was celebrated by many as a victory against racism. Do you think this was a red herring? That it actually paralyzed for a long time the left, including African Americans involved in the fight for a fairer world?

Many of the assumptions regarding the significance of Obama's election are entirely wrong, especially those that depict a Black man in the US presidency as symbolizing the fall of the last barrier of racism. But I do think that the election itself was important, especially since most people—including most Black people—did not initially believe that it was possible to elect a Black person to the presidency. Young people effectively created a movement—or one should qualify this by saying that it was a cyber movement—that achieved what was supposed to be impossible.

The problem was that people who associated themselves with that movement did not continue to wield that collective power as pressure that might have compelled Obama to move in more progressive directions (for example, against a military surge in Afghanistan, toward a swift dismantling of [the detainment camp at] Guantánamo, toward a stronger health care plan). Even as we are critical of Obama, I think it is important to emphasize that we would not have been better off with Romney in the White House. What we have lacked over these last five years is not the right president, but rather well-organized mass movements.

How would you define "Black feminism"? And what role could it play in to-day's society?

Black feminism emerged as a theoretical and practical effort demonstrating that race, gender, and class are inseparable in the social worlds we inhabit. At the time of its emergence, Black women were frequently asked to choose whether the Black movement or the women's movement was most important. The response was that this was the wrong question. The more appropriate question was how to understand the intersections and interconnections between the two movements. We are still faced with the challenge of understanding the complex ways race, class, gender, sexuality, nation, and ability are intertwined—but also how we move beyond these categories to understand the interrelationships of ideas and processes that seem to be separate and unrelated. Insisting on the connections between struggles and racism in the US and struggles against the Israeli repression of Palestinians, in this sense, is a feminist process.

Do you think it is time for people to disengage completely from the main political parties and from this concept that our "leaders" call "representative democracy"? Engaging in such a corrupt and rotten system, governed by money and greed, gives it legitimacy, right? What about stopping this charade—stopping voting and starting to create something from the bottom up that is new and organic?

I certainly don't think existing political parties can constitute our primary arenas of struggle, but I do think that the electoral arena can be used as a terrain on which to organize. In the US, we have needed an independent political party for a very long time—an antiracist, feminist workers party. I also think you are absolutely right in identifying grassroots activism as being the most important ingredient of building radical movements.

The Arab world has undergone tremendous changes in the last few years, with ongoing revolutions taking place in many countries. We seem to celebrate this in the West without looking at what is happening in our own countries and the involvement of our "leaders" in the dictatorships of the Arab world. Don't you think it's also time for us to have our own revolutions in the West?

Perhaps we should reverse the demand. I think it is entirely appropriate for people in the Arab world to demand that those of us in the West prevent our governments from bolstering repressive regimes—and especially Israel. The so-called war on terror has done inestimable damage to the world, including the intensification of anti-Muslim racism in the United States, Europe, and Australia. As progressives in the Global North, we certainly have not acknowledged our major responsibilities in the continuation of military and ideological attacks on people in the Arab world.

You recently gave a talk in London about Palestine, G4S (Group 4 Security, the biggest private security group in the world), and the prison-industrial complex. Could you tell us how those three are linked?

Under the guise of security and the security state, G4S has insinuated itself into the lives of people all over the world—especially in Britain, the United States, and Palestine. This company is the third-largest private corporation in the world after Walmart and Foxconn, and is the largest private employer on the continent of Africa. It has learned how to profit from racism, anti-immigrant practices, and from technologies of punishment in Israel and throughout the world. G4S is directly responsible for the ways Palestinians experience political incarceration, as well as aspects of the apartheid wall, imprisonment in South Africa, prison-like schools in the United States, and the wall along the US-Mexico border. Surprisingly, we learned during the London meeting that G4S also operates sexual assault centers in Britain.

How profitable is the prison-industrial complex? You often have said it is the equivalent of "modern slavery."

The global prison-industrial complex is continually expanding, as can be seen from the example of G4S. Thus, one can assume that its profitability is rising. It has come to include not only public and private prisons (and public prisons, which are more privatized than one would think, are increasingly subject to the demands of profit) but also juvenile facilities, military prisons, and interrogation centers. Moreover, the most profitable sector of the private prison business is composed of immigrant detention centers. One can therefore understand why the most repressive anti-immigrant legislation in the United States was drafted by private prison companies as an undisguised attempt to maximize their profits.

Is a prison- or jail-free society a utopia, or is it possible? How would that work?

I do think that a society without prisons is a realistic future possibility, but in a transformed society, one in which people's needs, not profits, constitute the driving force. At the same time prison abolition appears as a utopian idea precisely because the prison and its bolstering ideologies are so deeply rooted in our contemporary world. There are vast numbers of people behind bars in the United States—some two and a half million—and imprisonment is increasingly used as a strategy of deflection of the underlying social problems—racism, poverty, unemployment, lack of education, and so on. These issues are never seriously addressed. It is only a matter of time before people begin to realize that the prison is a false solution. Abolitionist advocacy can and should occur in relation to demands for quality education, for antiracist job strategies, for free health care, and within other progressive movements. It can help promote an anticapitalist critique and movements toward socialism.

What does the booming of the prison-industrial complex say about our society?

The soaring numbers of people behind bars all over the world and the increasing profitability of the means of holding them captive is one of the most dramatic examples of the destructive tendencies of global capitalism. But the obscene profits obtained from mass incarceration are linked to profits from the health care industry and from education and other commodified human services that actually should be freely available to everyone.

There is a scene in The Black Power Mixtape, *a documentary film about the Black Panther/Black Power movement that came out a couple years ago, in which the journalist asks you if you approve of violence. You answer, "Ask me——if I approve of violence!? This does not make any sense." Could you elaborate?*

I was attempting to point out that questions about the validity of violence should have been directed to those institutions that held and continue to hold a monopoly on violence: the police, the prisons, the military. I explained that I grew up in the US South at a time when the Ku Klux Klan was permitted by governments to engage in terrorist assaults against Black communities. At the time I was in jail, having been falsely charged with murder, kidnapping, and conspiracy and turned into a target of institutional violence, I was the one being asked whether I agreed with violence. Very bizarre. I was also attempting to point out that advocacy of revolutionary transformation was not primarily about violence, but about substantive issues like better life conditions for poor people and people of color.

Today, many people think you were a Black Panther, and some even think that you were one of the founding members. Could you explain, exactly, what was your role, what were your affiliations at that time?

I was not a founding member of the Black Panther Party. I was studying in Europe in 1966, the year that the BPP was founded. After I joined the Communist Party in 1968, I also became a member of the Black Panther Party and worked with a branch of the organization in Los Angeles, where I was in charge of political education. However, at one point the leadership decided that members of the BPP could not be affiliated with other parties, at which point I chose to retain my affiliation with the Communist Party. However, I continued to support and to work with the BPP. When I went to jail, the Black Panther Party was a major force advocating for my freedom.

Coming back to your answer about violence, when I heard what you said in the documentary, I thought about Palestine. The international community and the Western media are always asking, as a precondition, that Palestinians stop the violence. How would you explain the popularity of this narrative that the oppressed have to ensure the safety of the oppressors?

Placing the question of violence at the forefront almost inevitably serves to obscure the issues that are at the center of struggles for justice. This occurred in South Africa during the antiapartheid struggle. Interestingly Nelson Mandela—who has been sanctified as the most important peace advocate of our time—was kept on the US terrorist list until 2008. The important issues in the Palestinian struggle for freedom and self-determination are minimized and rendered invisible by those who try to equate Palestinian resistance to Israeli apartheid with terrorism.

When were you last in Palestine? What impression did your visit leave on you?

I traveled to Palestine in June 2011 with a delegation of indigenous and women of color feminist scholar/activists. The delegation included women who had grown up under South African apartheid, in the Jim Crow South, and on Indian reservations. Even though we had all been previously involved in Palestine solidarity activism, all of us were utterly shocked by what we saw and we resolved to encourage our constituencies to join the BDS (boycott, divestment, and sanctions) movement and to help intensify the campaign for a free Palestine. Most recently some of us were involved in the successful passage of a resolution urging participation in the academic and cultural boycott by the American Studies Association. Also, members of the delegation were involved in the passage of a resolution by the Modern Language Association censuring Israel for denying US academics entry to the West Bank in order to teach and do research at Palestinian universities.

There are various means of resistance available to people who are oppressed by racist or colonial regimes or foreign occupations (that is, according to the Additional Protocol I of the Geneva Conventions), including through the use of armed force. Nowadays, the Palestine solidarity movement has committed itself to the route of nonviolent resistance. Do you think this alone will end Israeli apartheid?

Solidarity movements are, of course, by their very nature nonviolent. In South Africa, even as an international solidarity movement was being organized, the ANC (African National Congress) and the SACP (South African Communist Party) came to the conclusion that they needed an armed wing of their movement: Umkhonto We Sizwe. They had every right to make that decision. Likewise, it is up to the Palestinian people to employ the methods they deem most likely to succeed in their struggle. At the same time, it is clear that if Israel is isolated politically and economically, as the BDS campaign is striving to do, Israel could not continue to implement its apartheid practices. If, for example, we in the United States could force the Obama administration to cease its $8 million-a-day support of Israel, this would go a long way toward pressuring Israel to end the occupation.

You are part of a committee for the release of Palestinian political prisoner Marwan Barghouti and all political prisoners. How important is it that they are all released?

It is essential that Marwan Barghouti and all political prisoners in Israeli jails are released. Barghouti has spent over two decades behind bars. His predicament reflects the fact that most Palestinian families have had at least one member imprisoned by the Israeli authorities. There are currently some five thousand Palestinian prisoners and we know that since 1967, eight hundred thousand Palestinians—40 percent of the male population—have been imprisoned by Israel. The demand to free all Palestinian political prisoners is a key ingredient of the demand to end the occupation.

You said during a talk at Birkbeck University that the Palestine issue needed to become a global one, a social issue that any movement fighting for justice should have on its program or agenda. What did you mean by that?

Just as the struggle to end South African apartheid was embraced by people all over the world and was incorporated into many social justice agendas, solidarity with Palestine must likewise be taken up by organizations and movements involved in progressive causes all over the world. The tendency has been to consider Palestine a separate—and unfortunately too often marginal—issue. This is precisely the moment to encourage everyone who believes in equality and justice to join the call for a free Palestine.

Is the struggle endless?

I would say that as our struggles mature, they produce new ideas, new issues, and new terrains on which we engage in the quest for freedom. Like Nelson Mandela, we must be willing to embrace the long walk toward freedom.

TWO

Ferguson Reminds Us
of the Importance
# of a Global Context

Interview by Frank Barat in Brussels (September 21, 2014)

Following what happened in Ferguson, what is your view of the framework of The New Jim Crow, *the book by Michelle Alexander?*

Michelle Alexander's book on mass incarceration appeared precisely at a moment that represented the peak of organizing against the prison-industrial complex. It became a best seller, and it popularized the struggle against mass incarceration, against the prison-industrial complex, in a very important way. Of course the argument that she makes about mass incarceration reinstituting some of the very strictures on civil rights that were fought for during the era of the mid-twentieth-century Black movement is very important.

Ferguson reminds us that we have to globalize our thinking about these issues. And if I were to be critical in a friendly way of the text, I would say that what it lacks is a global context, an international framework. And she herself points this out, so this is not something about which she is unaware. In many of her talks she explains that we also need this broader global context to understand the workings of the apparatus that has produced mass incarceration [in the United States].

Why do I say that Ferguson reminds us of the importance of a global context? What we saw in the police reaction to the resistance that spontaneously erupted in the aftermath of the killing of Michael Brown was an armed response that revealed the extent to which local police departments have been equipped with military arms, military technology, military training. The militarization of the police leads us to think about Israel and the militarization of the police there—if only the images of the police and not of the demonstrators had been shown, one might have assumed that Ferguson was Gaza. I think that it is important to recognize the extent to which, in the aftermath of the advent of the war on terror, police departments all over the US have been equipped with the means to allegedly "fight terror."

It's very interesting that during the commentary on Ferguson, someone pointed out that the purpose of the police is supposed to be to protect and serve. At least, that's their slogan. Soldiers are trained to shoot to kill. We saw the way in which that manifested itself in Ferguson.

I lived in London for ten years and every time you saw a cop in the street you got scared. They are technically "civil servants," but they do not fulfill this function. You talked about the US, the police being militarized—during the demonstrations for Gaza in France in Paris, it wasn't civil servants in the streets, it was riot police. Robocop-looking kind of people. This by itself creates and implies violence.

Precisely. That was the whole point. And also it might be important to point out that the Israeli police have been involved in the training of US police. So there is this connection between the US military and the Israeli military. And therefore it means that when we try to organize campaigns in solidarity with Palestine, when we try to challenge the Israeli state, it's not simply about focusing our struggles elsewhere, in another place. It also has to do with what happens in US communities.

We often talk here about the reproduction of the occupation: what's happening in Palestine is reproduced now in Europe, in the US, et cetera. It is important to make the link for people to understand how global the struggle is. But in your opinion is Ferguson an isolated incident?

Absolutely not. It's actually fortunate for those of us who are trying to participate in the building of a mass movement that some recent cases of police killings and vigilante killings have been widely publicized within the country as well as internationally. We had Trayvon Martin, which, of course, was just the tip of an iceberg. Michael Brown is just the tip of an iceberg. These kinds of confrontations and assaults and killings happen all of the time, all over the country in large as well as small cities. This is why it is a mistake to assume that these issues can be resolved on an individual level.

It is a mistake to assume that all we have to do is guarantee the prosecution of the cop who killed Michael Brown. The major challenge of this period is to infuse a consciousness of the structural character of state violence into the movements that spontaneously

arise . . . I don't know whether we can say yet that there is a movement, because movements are organized. But these spontaneous responses, which we know happen over and over again, will soon lead
to organizations and a continual movement.

*What does it say about the Black civil rights movement that more than fifty
years after MLK and Malcolm X, the targeting of Black people, Latinos/
Latinas, is still happening? Does that mean that the Black civil rights movement has failed or that it's a continuous struggle?*

The use of state violence against Black people, people of color,
has its origins in an era long before the civil rights movement—
in colonization and slavery. During the campaign around Trayvon
Martin, it was pointed out that George Zimmerman, a would-be
police officer, a vigilante, if you want to use that term, replicated
the role of slave patrols. Then as now the use of armed representa-
tives of the state was complemented by the use of civilians to perform the violence of the state.

So we don't have to stop at the era of the civil rights movement,
we can recognize that practices that originated with slavery were
not resolved by the civil rights movement. We may not experience
lynchings and Ku Klux Klan violence in the same way we did earlier,
but there still is state violence, police violence, military violence.
And to a certain extent the Ku Klux Klan still exists.

I don't think this means that the civil rights movement was un-
successful. The civil rights movement was very successful in what it
achieved: the legal eradication of racism and the dismantling of the
apparatus of segregation. This happened and we should not under-
estimate its importance. The problem is that it is often assumed that
the eradication of the legal apparatus is equivalent to the abolition

of racism. But racism persists in a framework that is far more expansive, far vaster than the legal framework.

Economic racism continues to exist. Racism can be discovered at every level in every major institution—including the military, the health care system, and the police.

It's not easy to eradicate racism that is so deeply entrenched in the structures of our society, and this is why it's important to develop an analysis that goes beyond an understanding of individual acts of racism and this is why we need demands that go beyond the prosecution of the individual perpetrators.

It reminds us obviously of South Africa, where legally apartheid was ended, but an economic apartheid, even sociological apartheid, is still in place. When we were in Cape Town for the Russell Tribunal, I was shocked to see people of color waiting every morning at the corner of the street to be picked up by employers who deemed to pay them three dollars an hour, I was horrified by the ghettos and shantytowns. You drive around the nicest beaches of Cape Town and a few minutes later it's like being in Mumbai or something.

Well, what's also interesting in South Africa is the fact that many of the positions of leadership from which Black people were of course totally excluded during apartheid are now occupied by Black people, including within the police hierarchy. I recently saw a film on the Marikana miners, who were attacked, injured, and many killed by the police. The miners were Black, the police force was Black, the provincial head of the police force was a Black woman. The national head of the police force is a Black woman. Nevertheless, what happened in Marikana was, in many important respects, a reenactment of Sharpeville. Racism is so dangerous because it does not necessarily depend on individual actors, but rather is deeply embedded in the apparatus . . .

And once you're in the apparatus . . .

Yes. And it doesn't matter that a Black woman heads the national police. The technology, the regimes, the targets are still the same. I fear that if we don't take seriously the ways in which racism is embedded in structures of institutions, if we assume that there must be an identifiable racist . . .

The "bad apples" type of . . .

. . . who is the perpetrator, then we won't ever succeed in eradicating racism.

You were a pioneer thinking along the lines of intersectionality. How has your thinking evolved?

Of course intersectionality—or efforts to think, analyze, organize as we recognize the interconnections of race, class, gender, sexuality—has evolved a great deal over the last decades. I see my work as reflecting not an individual analysis, but rather a sense within movements and collectives that it was not possible to separate issues of race from issues of class and issues of gender. There were many pioneers of intersectionality but I do think it is important to acknowledge an organization that existed in New York in the late sixties and seventies called the Third World Women's Alliance. That organization published a newspaper entitled *Triple Jeopardy*. Triple jeopardy was racism, sexism, and imperialism. Of course, imperialism reflected an international awareness of class issues. Many formations were attempting to bring these issues together.

My own book *Women, Race and Class* was one of many that were published during that era, including, to name only a few, *This Bridge Called My Back*, edited by Gloria Anzaldúa and Cherríe Moraga, the work of bell hooks and Michelle Wallace, and the anthology *All the Women Are White, All the Blacks Are Men, but Some of Us Are Brave: Black Women's Studies*.

So behind this concept of intersectionality is a rich history of struggle. A history of conversations among activists within movement formations, and with and among academics as well. I mention this genealogy that takes seriously the epistemological productions of those whose primary work is organizing radical movements because I think it's important to prevent the term "intersectionality" from erasing essential histories of activism. There were those of us who by virtue of our experience, not so much by virtue of academic analyses, recognized that we had to figure out a way to bring these issues together. They weren't separate in our bodies, but also they are not separate in terms of struggles.

I actually think that what is most interesting today, given that long history both of activism and all of the articles and books that have been written since then, what I think is most interesting is the conceptualization of the intersectionality of struggles. Initially intersectionality was about bodies and experiences. But now, how do we talk about bringing various social justice struggles together, across national borders? So we were talking about Ferguson and Palestine. How can we really create a framework that allows us to think these issues together and to organize around these issues together?

When we went to New York for the Russell Tribunal on Palestine session we tried to get support from Native Americans and the Black movement, but it proved very hard. We were eight hundred people in the audience. Maybe 5 percent were people of color.

But you can't simply invite people to join you and be immediately on board, particularly when they were not necessarily represented during the earlier organizing processes. You have to develop organizing strategies so that people identify with the particular issue as their issue. This is why I was suggesting in response to the question about Michelle Alexander that these connections need to be made in the context of the struggles themselves. So as you are organizing against police crimes, against police racism, you always raise parallels and similarities in other parts of the world.

And not only similarities, but you talk about the structural connections. What is the connection between the way the US police forces train and are armed and Israeli police and military. . . . So when you popularize that, encourage people to think about that . . .

. . . in a global way . . .

. . . exactly. This is one of the reasons I think so many people began to identify with the struggle against apartheid in South Africa. It wasn't a sense of "Oh, we have to lend solidarity to these people over there in South Africa." It was because they began to see that we have a common . . . connection. If that's not created, no matter how much you appeal to people, no matter how genuinely you invite them to join you, they will continue to see the activity as yours, not theirs.

It's crucial to make this connection, right? For people to understand that we are all neighbors because otherwise that's where racism starts. When people think along the line that a Black person doesn't have the same genes as a white one . . .

One of the things I've been thinking about in relation to the need to diversify movements in solidarity with Palestine is that, the tendency is to approach issues about which one is passionate within a narrow framework. People do this whatever their concerns are. But especially with the Palestine solidarity movement. My experience has been that many people assume that in order to be involved with Palestine, you have to be an expert.

So people are afraid to join because they say, "I don't understand. It's so complicated." Then they hear someone who is truly an expert, who does indeed represent the movement, who is so thoroughly informed about the history of the conflict, who speaks about the failure of the Oslo Accords, et cetera, when this happened and why it's important, but too often people feel that they are not sufficiently informed to consider themselves an advocate of justice in Palestine. The question is how to create windows and doors for people who believe in justice to enter and join the Palestine solidarity movement.

So that the question of how to bring movements together is also a question of the kind of language one uses and the consciousness one tries to impart. I think it's important to insist on the intersectionality of movements. In the abolition movement, we've been trying to find ways to talk about Palestine so that people who are attracted to a campaign to dismantle prisons in the US will also think about the need to end the occupation in Palestine. It can't be an afterthought. It has to be a part of the ongoing analysis.

Talking about the abolition movement, even with my kids, I've noticed when we're playing my little boy says, "Okay, well, if you're bad, you'll go to jail." And he's three and a half years old. So he is thinking bad = jail. This also applies to most people. So the idea of prison abolition must be a very hard one to advocate for. Where do you start? And how to you advocate for prison abolition versus prison reform?

The history of the very institution of the prison is a history of reform. Foucault points this out. Reform doesn't come after the advent of the prison; it accompanies the birth of the prison. So prison reform has always only created better prisons. In the process of creating better prisons, more people are brought under the surveillance of the correctional and law enforcement networks. The question you raise reveals the extent to which the site of the jail or prison is not only material and objective but it's ideological and psychic as well. We internalize this notion of a place to put bad people. That's precisely one of the reasons why we have to imagine the abolitionist movement as addressing those ideological and psychic issues as well. Not just the process of removing the material institutions or facilities.

Why is that person bad? The prison forecloses discussion about that. What is the nature of that badness? What did the person do? Why did the person do that? If we're thinking about someone who has committed acts of violence, why is that kind of violence possible? Why do men engage in such violent behavior against women? The very existence of the prison forecloses the kinds of discussions that we need in order to imagine the possibility of eradicating these behaviors.

Just send them to prison. Just keep on sending them to prison. Then of course, in prison they find themselves within a violent institution that reproduces violence. In many ways you can say that the institution feeds on that violence and reproduces it so that when the person is released he or she is probably worse.

So how does one persuade people to think differently? That's a question of organizing. In the United States, the abolitionist movement emerged around the late 196s and early '70s. The Quakers were very much a part of the emergence of the idea that we should consider abolishing imprisonment. The Quakers were present at the advent of the prison in the late eighteenth and early nineteenth centuries. They were the ones who originally thought the prison was a humane alternative to then-existing forms of punishment because it would allow people to be rehabilitated.

I would say that in the 1970s there was a moment when abolition was taken seriously. This was around the time of the Attica Rebellion, when people seriously began to think about—I'm talking about prominent lawyers and judges, journalists—began to think about something other than imprisonment. Of course eventually the pendulum swung in the opposite direction. That in a sense has been the history of the prison. On the one hand, there have been calls for changes, less violence, less repression, calls for reform and rehabilitation. But this never really worked. And so, on the other hand, there were calls for incapacitation and more punitive modes of control. All in all, the framework has always remained the same.

So the idea that I think animated people who were working toward the abolition of prisons is that we have to think about the larger context. We can't only think about crime and punishment. We can't only think about the prison as a place of punishment for those who have committed crimes. We have to think about the larger framework. That means asking: Why is there such a disproportionate number of Black people and people of color in prison? So we have to talk about racism. Abolishing the prison is about attempting to abolish racism. Why is there so much illiteracy? Why are so many prisoners illiterate? That means we have to attend to the educational system. Why is it that the three largest psychiatric institutions in the country are jails in New York, Chicago, Los Angeles: Rikers Island, Cook County Jail, and L.A. County Jail? That means we need to think about health care issues, and especially mental health care issues. We have to figure out how to abolish homelessness.

So it means you cannot think in such a narrow framework. This is what has, I think, permitted the jails and prisons to continue to grow and develop. Because we all have these ideas that somehow if you've committed a crime, then you need to be punished. So this is why we have tried to disarticulate crime and punishment in a popular sense by thinking about the "prison-industrial complex." Mike Davis was the first scholar/activist who used the term, especially with respect to the growing prison economy in California. The group that founded Critical Resistance thought that this would be a way for people to move away from that notion of bad people deserving punishment and to begin to ask questions about the economic, political, and ideological roles of the prison.

It's a big money-making business.

It's totally a money-making business.

They do need prisoners, right?

Absolutely. Especially given the increasing privatization of prisons, but there is privatization beyond private prisons. It consists of the outsourcing of prison services to all kinds of private corporations, and these corporations want larger prison populations. They want more bodies. They want more profits. And then you look at the way in which politicians always note that, whether there is a high crime rate or not, law-and-order rhetoric will always help to mobilize the voting population.

It makes you think about laws as well. I remember when I was in Australia talking to aboriginal people there was this law in central Australia that in practice meant "three strikes, you're out." Three strikes could be you stealing a loaf of bread one day, that's one strike; you stealing a pen, that's two strikes; you stealing another pen, that's three strikes. Some aboriginals are in jail for these type of strikes. You first think that it's crazy, but then realize that a lot of people are in jail for really minor offenses.

Well, I think that you can say that all over the world now the institution of the prison serves as a place to warehouse people who represent major social problems. Just as there is a disproportionate number of Black people in US prisons, there is an equally disproportionate number of aboriginal people behind bars in Australia. Getting rid of the people, putting them in prison is a way not to have to deal with immigration in Europe. Immigration, of course, happens as a result of all the economic changes that have happened globally—global capitalism, the restructuring of economies in countries of the Global South that makes it impossible for people to live there. In many ways you can say that the prison serves as an institution that consolidates the state's inability and refusal to address the most pressing social problems of this era.

I am thinking again about the abolitionist movement, which is about a better society. It's not only about prison abolition, it's about much more than that.

It is about prison abolition; it also inherits the notion of abolition from W. E. B. Du Bois who wrote about the abolition of slavery. He pointed out the end of slavery per se was not going to solve the myriad problems created by the institution of slavery. You could remove the chains, but if you did not develop the institutions that would allow for the incorporation of previously enslaved people into a democratic society, then slavery would not be abolished. In a sense, what we are arguing is that the prison abolitionist struggle follows the anti-slavery abolitionist struggle of the nineteenth century; the struggle for an abolitionist democracy is aspiring to create the institutions that will truly allow for a democratic society.

What about prisoners in prison? Can you talk about agency and struggles, prisoners and their own struggles?

Whenever you conceptualize social justice struggles, you will always defeat your own purposes if you cannot imagine the people around whom you are struggling as equal partners. Therefore if, and this is one of the problems with all of the reform movements, if you think of the prisoners simply as the objects of the charity of others, you defeat the very purpose of antiprison work. You are constituting them as an inferior in the process of trying to defend their rights.

The abolitionist movement has learned that without the actual participation of prisoners, there can be no campaign. That is a matter of fact. Many prisoners have contributed to the development of this consciousness: the abolition of the prison-industrial complex. It may not always be easy to guarantee the participation of prisoners, but without their participation and without acknowledging them as equals, we are bound to fail.

As you were referring to the need to ensure that there are women represented, you have to go a little bit further. I can give you some examples. Prisoners are able to make collect calls and so therefore how do you allow prisoners to participate in meetings? It doesn't really take very much technology to rig up an amplification

apparatus to a telephone and have people call in. I did an event on
Mumia Abu-Jamal. I was on stage with a telephone. Mumia called
in and he was able to address the entire audience. We have to think
about those processes.

I work with a women's prison organization in Australia directed
by Debbie Kilroy called Sisters Inside. Whenever I go to Australia,
and I'm about to go now, we always go into the prison because a good
portion of the leadership of the organization is in prison. It's so easy
to just forget, to think about the prison and its population abstractly.
If you're serious about developing egalitarian relations, you will figure out how to make these connections. How to stay in touch with
people behind bars. How to allow their voices to be heard.

*One cannot be lazy. How do we do that? How do we win men to fight for
women's liberation? How do we win whites to struggle against racism and for
the emancipation of people of color? It's the same thinking, right?*

Well, it is. We have to extricate ourselves from narrow identi-
tarian thinking if we want to encourage progressive people to embrace these struggles as their own. With respect to feminist struggles, men will have to do a lot of the important work. I often like
to talk about feminism not as something that adheres to bodies, not
as something grounded in gendered bodies, but as an approach—as
a way of conceptualizing, as a methodology, as a guide to strategies
for struggle. That means that feminism doesn't belong to anyone
in particular. Feminism is not a unitary phenomenon, so that increasingly there are men who are involved in feminist studies, for
example. As a professor I see increasing numbers of men majoring
in feminist studies, which is a good thing. In the abolitionist movement I see particularly young men who have a very rich feminist

perspective, and so how does one guarantee that that will happen? It will not happen without work. Both men and women—and trans persons—have to do that work, but I don't think it's a question of women inviting men to struggle. I think it's about a certain kind of consciousness that has to be encouraged so that progressive men are aware that they have a certain responsibility to bring in more men. Men can often talk to men in a different way. It's important for those who we might want to bring into the struggle to look at models. What does it mean to model feminism as a man? I tour the campuses regularly, and I was speaking at the University of Southern Illinois during a Black History Month celebration and I came into contact with this group of young men who are members of a group they call "Alternative Masculinities" and I was totally impressed by them. They work with the women's center. They have been trained in how to do rape crisis calls. They were really seriously engaging in all of that kind of activism that you assume that only women do. And then I remembered that many years ago in the 1970s there were a couple of men's formations like Men against Rape, Black Men against Rape, Against Domestic Violence, and I remember thinking then that it's just a matter of time before this gets taken up by men all over. But it never really happened. So I was reminded by these young men in "Alternative Masculinities" that after all of these decades they should today represent a far more popular trend. But this is the kind of thing that needs to be happening.

It doesn't happen by itself. It doesn't happen automatically. You have to intervene. You have to make conscious interventions.

About the death penalty. Is there actually a chance to abolish it at the state level in the United States?

Well, fortunately, there are some signs that it might be possible to abolish the death penalty in New York, for example. Of course, there have been moments in certain states that it almost feels like we're on the verge of abolishing the death penalty, and then it doesn't happen; even if people are not executed, it remains on the books. When Troy Davis was killed, on September 21, 2011, there was an international movement. People were convinced that the state of Georgia was not going to execute him. But they did. I don't know whether we are ever going to abolish the death penalty without a mass movement. And the state-by-state approach may take far too long.

But at the same time I should say that oftentimes a particular conjunctural set of conditions will arise, a particular conjuncture, and it reveals the opportunity to accomplish something. For example when the Occupy movement emerged in 2011, that was a really exciting moment. Had we previously done the organizing that would have allowed us to take advantage of that moment, we could have really used that opportunity to build, organize formations—whether we're talking about party formations [or not]—and we would have a much stronger anticapitalist movement today. I think that moment was important because it did provide an opportunity to develop a critique of capitalism that had not previously been popularized, and now we talk about the "99 percent" and the "1 percent"—that's a part of our vocabulary.

. . . changing the narrative . . .

Yes. Sometimes we have to do the work even though we don't yet see a glimmer on the horizon that it's actually going to be possible.

The groundwork has to be done on a daily basis . . .

The prison abolitionist movement is also incorporating demands for the abolition of the death penalty. We need to develop broader resistance to the death penalty. In the case of Mumia it worked on a small scale—he was removed from death row, but we should have been able to use that as a launching pad for Mumia's full freedom, for abolition of the death penalty, and, of course also of prisons. Capital punishment remains a central issue. We need to popularize understandings of how racism underwrites the death penalty, and so many other institutions. The death penalty is about structural racism and it incorporates historical memories of slavery. We cannot understand why the death penalty continues to exist in the United States in the way that it does, without an analysis of slavery. So this is again one of the really important issues confronting us. But I think we will need a mass movement and a global movement to finally remove the death penalty from the books.

THREE

We Have to Talk about Systemic Change

Interview by Frank Barat in Paris (December 10, 2014)

The last time we spoke about Ferguson, the crime had happened, but the grand jury had not given its verdict yet. Following the death of another Black man, Eric Garner, at the hands of police, I'd like to talk about it again. Two Black men died and the cops are walking free. What needs to change?

First, I would point out that police killings of Black men and women are not unusual. Robin D. G. Kelley wrote an article recently, which you might find interesting. You can find it on the Portside website. The name of the article is "Why We Won't Wait." The article lists all of the Black people who had been killed by police, while we were waiting to hear the results of the Ferguson verdict.

These killings all took place in a couple of months?

Exactly—during the time the grand jury was in session listening to evidence. I think that we often treat these cases as if they were exceptions, as if they were aberrations. Whereas in actuality they happen all the time. And we assume that if we are only able to punish the perpetrator, then justice will have been done. But as a matter of fact, as horrendous as it was that the grand jury refused to indict two police officers for the killings of Michael Brown and Eric Garner, had they indicted the officers, I don't know whether anything would have changed. I'm making this point in order to emphasize that even when police are indicted, we cannot be certain that change is on the agenda.

There is a case in North Carolina, I believe, involving a young man by the name of Jonathan Ferrell, who was killed by the police after he had an accident with his automobile and attempted to get help by knocking on someone's door. The person apparently claimed that he might have been a burglar and called the police, who immediately killed him. Now in that case the policeman was not initially indicted; however, the prosecutor persisted and eventually the grand jury did indict him. I guess the point I'm making is, we have to talk about systemic change. We can't be content with individual actions.

And so that means a whole range of things. That means reconceptualizing the role that the police play. That means perhaps establishing community control of the police. Not simply a review of actions in the aftermath of a crime by the police, but community bodies that have the power to actually control and dictate the actions of the police. That means addressing racism in the larger sense. It means also, looking at the ways in which police are encouraged to use violence as a first resort and the connection between this institutionalized violence and other modes of violence. In relation to Ferguson, especially, it means demilitarization of the police as a demand that needs to be taken up all over the country.

So we are talking about a systemic change, right?
    Exactly.

Deep down in the system.
    Yes, absolutely.

*You mentioned this Black man whose car had broken down, looking for help,
and the people pretty much straight away thought he was a burglar or something. Do you think this has to do with stereotypes, the way that society and
the media portray Black people as potentially dangerous, potentially criminal . . . creating this image in people's minds, creating prejudice?*

    Yes, absolutely. And as a matter of fact, these stereotypes have
been functioning since the era of slavery. Frederick Douglass
wrote about the tendency to impute crime to color. He pointed
out that a white man in Black face committed a whole range of
crimes because he knew well that he would not be suspected by
virtue of the fact that he was white. On the other hand all Black
people were subject to the ideological link between Blackness and
criminalization.

    Racism, as it has evolved in the history of the United States, has
always involved a measure of criminalization so that it is not difficult
to understand how stereotypical assumptions about Black people
being criminals persist to this day. Racial profiling is an example.
The fact that driving while Black can be dangerous. Recently, one
of the trending Twitter conversations had to do with "criming while
White." A whole number of white people wrote in and described
crimes they had committed for which they were never suspected,
and one person pointed out that he and a Black friend were arrested
by the police for stealing a candy bar. The cop gave the white person

the candy bar, and the Black person was eventually sentenced to prison.

This is true everywhere in a way. There is profiling in Paris, too. If you talk to someone who is of Moroccan or Algerian descent in Paris, they face pretty much the same stereotypes and fabrications as African Americans in the USA. Why do you think those stereotypes are fabricated? Is it a case of "divide and rule" strategy?

You know, racism is a very complex phenomenon. There are very important structural elements of racism and it's often those structural elements that aren't taken into consideration when there is discussion about ending racism or challenging racism. There's also the impact on the psyche, and this is where the persistence of stereotypes comes in. The ways in which over a period of decades and centuries Black people have been dehumanized, that is to say represented as less than human, and so the representational politics that one sees through the media, that one sees in other modes of communication, that come into play in social interactions, have equated Black with criminal. And so it is not difficult to understand how they have persisted so long.

The question is, why there has not been up until now a serious effort to understand the impact of racism on institutions and on individual attitudes? Until we are able to address racism in that kind of comprehensive way, the stereotypes will persist.

What about Obama? He didn't visit Ferguson, not yet anyway. How does he fit in the political picture at the moment?

Well I think that one explanation—one of a number of explanations for the rise of a very interesting foundation for a movement against racism and racist violence and police violence as we are witnessing at this very moment—has to do with the fact that the election of Obama was hailed as the possible beginning of a so-called postracial era. Of course it didn't make a great deal of sense that the election of one person could transform the impact of racism on institutions and attitudes of an entire country. But I do think that the fact that there is now a sitting Black president renders the racism, the racist violence that people have witnessed, renders that violence more impactful. And no, Obama did not visit Ferguson. Eric Holder did, the attorney general, and as critical as I may be of that administration, I think it was important that Eric Holder pointed out, at least early on, that the militarization of the police was an important issue. Initially in Ferguson we saw the military garb, the military equipment. Interestingly enough during the last period we haven't had visual images that emphasized the fact that the police had been the recipients of military garb, weaponry, technology, et cetera.

Anyway I don't think we can rely on governments, regardless of who is in power, to do the work that only mass movements can do. I think what is most important about the sustained demonstrations that are now happening is that they are having the effect of refusing to allow these issues to die.

You mentioned that one person will not change the whole system, so how is Obama constrained by the system that actually got him elected?

Well of course, there is a whole apparatus that controls the presidency that is absolutely resistant to change. Which isn't to excuse Obama from taking bolder steps. I think that there are steps that he could have taken had he insisted. But if one looks at the history of struggles against racism in the US, no change has ever happened simply because the president chose to move in a more progressive direction.

Every change that has happened has come as a result of mass movements—from the era of slavery, the Civil War, and the involvement of Black people in the Civil War, which really determined the outcome. Many people are under the impression that it was Abraham Lincoln who played the major role, and he did as a matter of fact help to accelerate the move toward abolition, but it was the decision on the part of slaves to emancipate themselves and to join the Union Army—both women and men—that was primarily responsible for the victory over slavery. It was the slaves themselves and of course the abolitionist movement that led to the dismantling of slavery. When one looks at the civil rights era, it was those mass movements—anchored by women, incidentally—that pushed the government to bring about change. I don't see why things would be any different today.

So do you think Ferguson can be the catalyst for a new movement? Could this be the tipping point?

I do think that movements require time to develop and mature. They don't happen spontaneously. They occur as a result of organizing and hard work that most often happens behind the scenes. Over the last two decades I would say, there has actually been sustained organizing against police violence, racism, racist police violence, against prisons, the prison-industrial complex, and I think that the sustained protests we are seeing now have a great deal to do with that organizing. They reflect the fact that the political consciousness in so many communities is so much higher than people think. That there is a popular understanding of the connection between racist police violence and systemic issues. The prison-industrial complex has something to do with the CIA's use of secret prisons and the torture that was recently revealed. So I think that we have a foundation for a movement. I won't say that there exists an organized movement because we haven't yet reached that point, but there's a powerful foundation and people are ready for a movement.

Talking about the prison-industrial complex and the prison abolition movement in the US, what can movements nowadays accomplish? What lessons did we learn from the sixties and seventies?

Well, I think we learned in the sixties and the seventies that mass movements can indeed bring about systematic change. If one looks at all of the legislation that was passed, the Civil Rights Act, for example, the Voting Rights Act, that did not happen as a result of a president taking extraordinary steps. It happened as a result of people marching and organizing.

I can remember that in 1963 during the civil rights era, before the March on Washington that summer, in Birmingham, Alabama, there was a children's crusade. Children were organized to face the high-power firehoses and the police, Bull Connor's police in Birmingham. Of course, there were some who disagreed with allowing the children to participate at that level; even Malcolm X thought it was not appropriate to expose children to that amount of danger, but the children wanted to participate. And the images of children facing police dogs and firehoses circulated all over the world and that helped to create a global consciousness of the brutality of racism. It was an extraordinary step. And this is something that's often forgotten, the role that children actually played in breaking the stronghold of silence regarding racism.

So I guess during the sixties and seventies we did really learn that change was possible. Not, ultimately, the kind of change we really wanted. I shouldn't put it that way. I should say not enough change because change did occur within the sphere of the law, which was extremely important. But we did not experience the economic change and other modes of structural change that we will need in order to begin to root out racism.

That's the thing. How can movements pressure even the most reluctant politicians?

Well, Lyndon B. Johnson, who was the president during that era—he was a reluctant southern politician who clearly assented to racism. But it was under his administration that important laws were passed. So I think movements can indeed force reluctant politicians to take steps. If one looks at the example of South Africa, who would have ever believed that de Klerk would take the position he ended up taking? That was because of the movements within South Africa, the South African movement outside of South Africa, and also the global solidarity campaign.

Staying on the US side, what's the future of Black politics?

Well, I don't know whether Obama played a major role in developing the future of Black politics within the US. But I think the real question is about the future of antiracist politics.

You touched on it before, the fact that Obama was elected maybe actually was a block somehow . . .

Actually, I think it's important to conceptualize Black politics in a broader framework now. We can't think about Black politics in the same way that we once thought about it. What I would say is that in many ways the Black struggle in the US serves as an emblem of the struggle for freedom. It's emblematic of larger struggles for freedom. So within the sphere of Black politics, I would also have to include gender struggles, struggles against homophobia, and I would also have to include struggles against repressive immigration policies. I think it's important to point to what is often called the Black radical tradition. And the Black radical tradition is related not simply to Black people but to all people who are struggling for freedom. So the future in that respect I think, has to be considered open. Certainly Black freedom in the narrow sense has not yet been won. Particularly considering the fact that huge numbers of Black people are ensconced in poverty. Considering the fact that a hugely disproportionate number of Black people are now in prison, caught in the web of the prison-industrial complex, but at the same time we have to look at Latino populations, and we have to look at indigenous populations, Native American people. We have to look at the way in which anti-Muslim racism has really thrived on the foundation of anti-Black racism. So it's far more complicated now and I would never argue that it's possible to look at Black freedom in a narrow sense. And particularly given the fact that we have the emergence of a Black middle class, the fact that Obama is the president is emblematic of the rise of Black individuals, not only within politics but also within the economic hierarchies. And that is not going to necessarily transform the condition of the majority of Black people.

I think that's very interesting. I'm not sure how to put it, but do you think that when a group of people, and I mean the example of South Africa is telling as well, gets to high places in terms of politics or business, money then comes before Blackness or the fact of being Native American? I was in Chile recently and the Palestinian community in Chile is one of the largest in the world. There are something like 450,000 Palestinians in Chile . . .

Oh, I didn't know that.

While I was giving lectures in Chile, I visited Villa Grimaldi, where Pinochet tortured and killed many people. People told me that about 60 percent of the Palestinian community in Chile, which is one of the wealthiest in the world as well, supported Pinochet during the regime. Not because Pinochet tortured and killed people, but because Pinochet was a neoliberal. They were interested in keeping their wealth and privileges. So before condemning the torture they were looking at their wallets. The same happened in South Africa . . .

It's all very complicated and particularly during this era of global capitalism and neoliberalism. In South Africa the rise of a very powerful and very affluent Black sector of the population, a Black bourgeoisie if you will, the potential for which was never really taken into account, at least not publicly during the struggle against apartheid—it was assumed that once Black people achieved political and economic power, there would be economic freedom for everyone, and we see that that's not necessarily the case. We have basically the same situation in the US.

I've been actually visiting Brazil frequently for the last period, and Brazil is now on the cusp of some major breakthroughs with respect to racism. I think that they have the opportunity to choose whether to follow the example of the US and South Africa . . . so it surprises me that Palestinians would have been supportive of Pinochet, but I don't find it entirely unbelievable.

Not all of them, right . . .

No, you said 60 percent, which is substantial. And I think it's extremely important that over the last period we've seen the development of solidarity campaigns that have brought different struggles together. Palestinians who have been inspired by Black struggles in the US should inspire Black people to continue the struggle for freedom. But on the other hand, Palestinians perhaps can look at the problems inherent in the assumption that the rise of individual Black people to power can in fact change the whole situation. What is going to lead to freedom for the Palestinian people is going to be a lot more complicated than money.

What can Black feminism and the Black struggle offer to the Palestinian liberation movement?

I don't know whether I would phrase the question in that way, because I think that solidarity always implies a kind of mutuality. Given the fact that in the US we're already encouraged to assume that we have the best of everything, that US exceptionalism puts us in a situation as activists to offer advice to people struggling all over the world, and I don't agree with that—I think we share our experiences. Just as I think the development of Black feminism and women-of-color feminisms can offer ideas, experiences, analyses to Palestinians, so can Black feminisms and women-of-color feminisms learn from the struggle of the Palestinian people and Palestinian feminists. So I think that the whole notion of intersectionality that has characterized the kind of feminisms we're talking about, that we cannot simply look at gender in isolation from race, from class, from sexuality, from nationality, from ability, from a whole range of other issues that Palestinians, or people in the Palestinian struggle, have given expression to that and have actually helped people in the US imagine broader notions of intersectionality.

How has the Palestine struggle changed in the US over the last several years?

I feel some really important changes have occurred. For far too long the issue of Palestinian freedom has been marginalized. So much so that many people in the US have been progressive except for Palestine. And I take this from Rebecca Vilkomerson, who talks about PEPs, "Progressives Except Palestine." Now this is changing. The impact of the influence of Zionism, which used to be pervasive, is losing its force. On college campuses, all college and university campuses, Students for Justice in Palestine (SJP) has really grown and large numbers of people who are not necessarily Palestinian, who are not necessarily Arab or Muslim, have become active in the SJP groups. It is increasingly becoming, that is to say the issue of Palestine, is increasingly being incorporated into major social justice issues. And my own personal experience has been that in the past I could always expect resistance or challenges when talking about Palestine, but now this is become increasingly acceptable. And I think this has to do with what is happening in Palestine itself. It has to do with the rise of Palestine solidarity movements all over the world, not just in the US. It has to do specifically in the US with increasing numbers of people associated with Black, and Native American, and Latino movements incorporating Palestine into the agenda. I think I spoke in the last interview about the tweets of Palestinian activists used to provide advice for protesters in Ferguson, on how to deal with the tear gas, so that direct connection that has been facilitated by social media has been important as well.

I was in Sevilla recently for a conference, and Rahim Kurwa from SJP UCLA, which you know well, was there with me, and I told him I was going to meet you, and he had an interesting question for you in terms of student activism. He asked:"What is the role of student activism today, and how should students think about the relationship to the broader community and the movements that surround the campuses particularly in a time when universities are becoming increasingly elite institutions?"

Certainly, and historically UCLA has been the center of a whole number of struggles that are linked to the community. I can mention my own struggle at UCLA. But I think that now students who challenge the borders of the university and the attempt to establish universities as a stronghold of neoliberal elitism, those challenges are extremely important. With the case of SJP, linking campuses to BDS all over the country has not only had the effect of strengthening the BDS movement, but has opened up possibilities for students to challenge prison privatization, and of course on many of the campuses where there've been efforts to develop resolutions against corporations that profit from the occupation of Palestine, there have also been struggles for resolutions against companies that profit from prison privatization. So I think that these two are in many ways symbiotically connected. And that's one example of many.

In terms of Palestine, again in the US, how are the narratives similar or different from the antiapartheid days?

There are a lot of similarities, precisely because BDS has chosen to follow the root of the antiapartheid struggle toward a hopefully more global sense of solidarity by using the method of mass boycott. I guess what is different is the existence of a powerful

Zionist lobby. Certainly there was a powerful apartheid lobby, but it did not have nearly the influence as the Zionist lobby, which can be seen in terms of Black religion; its tentacles reach into the Black church, there have been direct efforts to, on the part of the state of Israel, to recruit significant Black figures. And I don't know whether we experienced that level of sophistication during the antiapartheid era. Certainly the Israeli state has learned from that movement. But at the same time I think that we've never seen on a grassroots level the kind of affinity with the struggle in Palestine as we are witnessing today among activist groups. And my experience has been whereas once one would have expected perhaps restrained enthusiasm for the Palestinian struggle, now one can expect that audiences everywhere embrace this struggle. The American Studies Association passed an important resolution on Palestine solidarity. Recently I had the opportunity to participate on a panel of the National Women's Studies Association (NWSA) conference, and the NWSA has never taken a position on Palestine due to Zionist influences, I would say. In a large plenary gathering with perhaps twenty-five hundred people, during a panel on Palestine, someone asked whether we could take a floor vote, whether people there wanted the NWSA to take a strong position in support of BDS, and virtually everyone in the audience stood up. This was so unprecedented. There may have been ten or twenty people sitting down, but the sustained applause, it was actually a very exciting to experience.

These changes are crucial to bring about a bigger one. I think MESA as well, the Middle East Studies Association, has recently endorsed the BDS call . . .

. . . even Israeli academics said this was a major change.

Well, let's remember that it was the Asian American Studies Association that first passed a resolution and then the American Studies Association that followed, and now of course . . .

MESA and . . .

. . . and Critical Ethnic Studies Association. Quite a number of academic organizations.

So it's all great, but in your opinion, what could we do to strengthen the pro-justice movement even more, in the US? And the same question applies to the whole world I think.

Well, I think that we constantly have to make connections. So that when we are engaged in the struggle against racist violence, in relation to Ferguson, Michael Brown, and New York, Eric Garner, we can't forget the connections with Palestine. So in many ways I think we have to engage in an exercise of intersectionality. Of always foregrounding those connections so that people remember that nothing happens in isolation. That when we see the police repressing protests in Ferguson we also have to think about the Israeli police and the Israeli army repressing protests in occupied Palestine.

We talked about the militarization of the police; you see it in Ferguson, you also see it in the West Bank, in Gaza—you also see it in Athens, in Greece, right now. Police forces looking like "Robocops," the fact that this is a global struggle becomes more obvious when you make those connections . . .

. . . But they're shrewd, so we no longer see it in Ferguson because they have decided to make their militarization less visible,

but even when we can't see it, we have to make the point. And I
think that's perhaps even more important that people learn to see
it through the efforts to render those military influences invisible.

*Talking about connections, do you see a role for yourself in connecting anti-
racist movements in the Arab world with Black consciousness and liberation
movements in the US?*

Well, I don't know whether I would talk about a specific role
for myself, an individual role, but certainly I would see myself par-
ticipating in the efforts to make those connections, to render those
connections more palpable and more visible. Oftentimes we learn
from movements; that happens at the grassroots level and we should
be very careful not to assume that these insights belong to ourselves
as individuals or at least as more visible figures, but we have to
recognize that we have learned from those moments and we want
to share those insights. That is the role I would see myself playing.

*Again, talking about Black feminism, what positive developments are you
seeing in Black feminism in the United States?*

Well, the embracing of the cause of Palestinian solidarity is
really important. Beverly Guy-Sheftall, who is a very important
figure in the development of Black feminism, who teaches at Spelman College, which is one of the historically Black educational
institutions . . .

Howard Zinn taught there . . .

Yes, he did. Alice Walker attended Spelman. It's a small wom-
en's college, but it is really important. And Beverly Guy-Sheftall
was a member of the same delegation that I joined to Palestine. It

was an indigenous and feminist-of-color, scholar-activist delegation to Palestine. And Beverly Guy-Sheftall is a very important figure who is so modest that she never claims any space for herself, but I would like to emphasize the importance of the role that she has played. Spelman College, which is a predominantly Black institution, has an SJP chapter, which is the only SJP chapter on a major HBCU and I think they're giving leadership to the other historically Black colleges and universities. So I think we can hope to see a great deal in the future. Beverly has been really consistent and persistent in foregrounding the Palestinian struggle.

Have you seen the consolidation of feminism in your lifetime that has effectively challenged both patriarchy and white-privilege liberal feminism, if we can call it that?

I think that movements, feminist movements, other movements are most powerful when they begin to affect the vision and perspective of those who do not necessarily associate themselves with those movements. So that the radical feminisms, or radical antiracist feminisms are important in the sense that they have affected the way especially young people think about social justice struggles today. That we cannot assume that it is possible to be victorious in any antiracist movement as long as we don't consider how gender figures in, how gender and sexuality and class and nationality figure into those struggles. It used to be the case that the struggles for freedom were seen to be male struggles. Freedom for Black people was equivalent to freedom for the Black man and if one looks at Malcolm X and many other figures, you see this constantly. But now this is no longer possible. And I think that feminism is not an approach that is or should be embraced simply by women but increasingly it has to be an approach embraced by people of all genders.

In terms of change, what is the most significant change in Black politics since the end of the civil rights movement? Is it related to Black feminism as well?

Well, I think the interconnectedness of antiracist movements with gender is crucial, but we also need to do this with class, nationality, and ethnicity—I don't think that we can imagine Black movements in the same way today as we once did. The assumption that Black freedom was freedom for the Black man created a certain kind of border around the Black struggle which can no longer exist. So I think that the Black radical tradition has to embrace the struggles against anti-Muslim racism, which is perhaps the most virulent form of racism today. It makes no sense to imagine eradicating anti-Black racism without also eradicating anti-Muslim racism.

Can there be policing and imprisonment in the US without racism?

At this point, at this moment in the history of the US I don't think that there can be policing without racism. I don't think that the criminal justice system can operate without racism. Which is to say that if we want to imagine the possibility of a society without racism, it has to be a society without prisons. Without the kind of policing that we experience today. I think that different frameworks, perhaps restorative justice frameworks, need to be invoked in order to begin to imagine a society that is secure. I think that security is a main issue, but not the kind of security that is based on policing and incarceration. Perhaps transformative justice provides a framework for imagining a very different kind of security in the future.

You've been an activist for decades. What keeps you going? Do you think we should remain optimistic about the future?

Well, I don't think we have any alternative other than remaining optimistic. Optimism is an absolute necessity, even if it's only optimism of the will, as Gramsci said, and pessimism of the intellect. What has kept me going has been the development of new modes of community. I don't know whether I would have survived had not movements survived, had not communities of resistance, communities of struggle survived. So whatever I'm doing I always feel myself directly connected to those communities and I think that this is an era where we have to encourage that sense of community particularly at a time when neoliberalism attempts to force people to think of themselves only in individual terms and not in collective terms. It is in collectivities that we find reservoirs of hope and optimism.

FOUR

On Palestine, G4S, and the Prison-Industrial Complex

Speech at SOAS in London (December 13, 2013)

When this event highlighting the importance of boycotting the transnational security corporation G4S was organized, we could not have known that it would coincide with the death and memorialization of Nelson Mandela.

As I reflect on the legacies of struggle we associate with Mandela, I cannot help but recall the struggles that helped to forge the victory of his freedom and thus the arena on which South African apartheid was dismantled. Therefore I remember Ruth First and Joe Slovo, Walter and Albertina Sisulu, Govan Mbeki, Oliver Tambo, Chris Hani, and so many others who are no longer with us. In keeping with Mandela's insistence of always locating himself within a context of collective struggle, it is fitting to evoke the names of a few of his comrades who played pivotal roles in the elimination of apartheid.

While it is moving to witness the unanimous and continued out-
pouring of praise for Nelson Mandela, it is important to question
the meaning of this sanctification. I know that he himself would
have insisted on not being elevated, as a single individual, to a sec-
ular sainthood, but rather would have always claimed space for his
comrades in the struggle and in this way would have seriously challenged the process of sanctification. He was indeed extraordinary,
but as an individual he was especially remarkable because he railed
against the individualism that would single him out at the expense
of those who were always at his side. His profound individuality
resided precisely in his critical refusal to embrace the individualism
that is such a central ideological component of neoliberalism.

I therefore want to take the opportunity to thank the countless
numbers of people here in the UK, including the many then-exiled
members of the ANC and the South African Communist Party, who
built a powerful and exemplary antiapartheid movement in this
country. Having traveled here on numerous occasions during the
1970s and the 1980s to participate in antiapartheid events, I thank
the women and men who were as unwavering in their commitment
to freedom as was Nelson Mandela. Participation in such solidarity
movements here in the UK was as central to my own political for-
mation as were the movements that saved my life.

As I mourn the passing of Nelson Mandela I offer my deep grat-
itude to all of those who kept the antiapartheid struggle alive for
so many decades, for all the decades that it took to finally rid the
world of the racism and repression associated with the system of
apartheid. And I evoke the spirit of the South African Constitution
and its opposition to racism and anti-Semitism as well as to sexism
and homophobia.

This is the context within which I join with you once more to intensify campaigns against another regime of apartheid and in solidarity with the struggles of the Palestinian people. As Nelson Mandela said, "We know too well that our freedom is incomplete without the freedom of the Palestinians."

Mandela's political emergence occurred within the context of an internationalism that always urged us to make connections among freedom struggles, between the Black struggle in the southern United States and the African liberation movements—conducted by the ANC in South Africa, the MPLA in Angola, SWAPO in Namibia, FRELIMO in Mozambique, and PAIGC in Guinea Bissau and Cape Verde. These international solidarities were not only among people of African descent but with Asian and Latin American struggles as well, including ongoing solidarity with the Cuban revolution and solidarity with the people struggling against US military aggression in Vietnam.

A half-century later we have inherited the legacies of those solidarities—however well or however badly specific struggles may have concluded—as what produced hope and inspiration and helped to create real conditions to move forward.

We are now confronted with the task of assisting our sisters and brothers in Palestine as they battle against Israeli apartheid today. Their struggles have many similarities with those against South African apartheid, one of the most salient being the ideological condemnation of their freedom efforts under the rubric of terrorism. I understand that there is evidence indicating historical collaboration between the CIA and the South African apartheid government—in fact, it appears that it was a CIA agent who gave SA authorities the location of Nelson Mandela's whereabouts in 1962, leading directly to his capture and imprisonment.

Moreover, it was not until the year 2008—only five years ago—that Mandela's name was taken off the terrorist watch list, when George W. Bush signed a bill that finally removed him and other members of the ANC from the list. In other words when Mandela visited the US after his release in 1990, and when he later visited as South Africa's president, he was still on the terrorist list and the requirement that he be banned from the US had to be expressly waived.

The point I am making is that for a very long time, Mandela and his comrades shared the same status as numerous Palestinian leaders and activists today and that just as the US explicitly collaborated with the SA apartheid government, it continues to support the Israeli occupation of Palestine, currently in the form of over $8.5 million a day in military aid. We need to let the Obama administration know that the world knows how deeply the US is implicated in the occupation.

It is an honor to participate in this meeting, especially as one of the members of the International Political Prisoners Committee calling for the freedom of Palestinian political prisoners, recently formed in Cape Town, and also as a member of the jury of the Russell Tribunal on Palestine. I would like to thank War on Want for sponsoring this meeting and progressive students, faculty, and workers at SOAS, for making it possible for us to be here this evening.

This evening's gathering specifically focuses on the importance of expanding the BDS movement—the boycott, divestment, and sanctions movement called for by Palestinian civil society—which has been crafted along the lines of the powerful model of the anti-apartheid movement with respect to South Africa. While there numerous transnational corporations have been identified as targets of the boycott, Veolia for example, as well as Sodastream, Ahava, Caterpillar, Boeing, Hewlett Packard, and others, we are focusing our attention this evening on G4S.

G4S is especially important because it participates directly and blatantly in the maintenance and reproduction of repressive appa-ratuses in Palestine—prisons, checkpoints, the apartheid wall, to name only a few examples. G4S represents the growing insistence on what is called "security" under the neoliberal state and ideologies of security that bolster not only the privatization of security but the privatization of imprisonment, the privatization of warfare, as well as the privatization of health care and education.

G4S is responsible for the repressive treatment of political pris-oners inside Israel. Through Addameer, directed by Sahar Francis, we have learned about the terrifying universe of torture and impris-onment which is faced by so many Palestinians but also about their hunger strikes and other forms of resistance.

G4S is the third-largest private corporation in the world—be-hind Walmart, which is the largest, and Foxconn, the second larg-est. On the G4S website, one discovers that the company represents itself as capable of providing protection for a broad range of "people and property," from rock stars and sports stars to "ensuring that travelers have a safe and pleasant experience in ports and airports around the world to secure detention and escorting of people who are not lawfully entitled to remain in a country."

"In more ways than you might realize," the website reads, "G4S is securing your world." We might add that in more ways that we real-ize, G4S has insinuated itself into our lives under the guise of security and the security state—from the Palestinian experience of political incarceration and torture to racist technologies of separation and

apartheid; from the wall in Israel to prison-like schools in the US and
the wall along the US-Mexico border. G4S-Israel has brought sophisticated technologies of control to HaSharon prison, which includes
children among its detainees, and Damun prison, which incarcerates
women.

Against this backdrop, let us explore the deep involvement of
G4S in the global prison-industrial complex. I am not only referring
to the fact that the company owns and operates private prisons all
over the world, but that it is helping to blur the boundary between
schools and jails. In the US schools in poor communities of color
are thoroughly entangled with the security state, so much so that
sometimes we have a hard time distinguishing between schools and
jails. Schools look like jails; schools use the same technologies of
detection as jails and they sometimes use the same law enforcement
officials. In the US some elementary schools are actually patrolled
by armed officers. As a matter of fact, a recent trend among school
districts that cannot afford security companies like G4S has been to
offer guns and target practice to teachers. I kid you not.

But G4S, whose major proficiencies are related to security, is
actually involved in the operation of schools. A website entitled
"Great Schools" includes information on Central Pasco Girls Academy in Florida, which is represented as a small alternative public
school. If you look at the facilities page of the G4S website you
will discover this entry: "Central Pasco Girls Academy serves mod-
erate-risk females, ages 13-18, who have been assessed as need-
ing intensive mental health services." G4S indicates that they use
"gender-responsive services" and that they address sexual abuse and
substance abuse, et cetera. While this may sound relatively innocu-
ous, it is actually a striking example of the extent to which security

has found its way into the educational system, and thus also of the way education and incarceration have been linked under the sign of capitalist profit. This example also demonstrates that the reach of the prison-industrial complex is far beyond the prison.

This company that provides "security" for numerous agencies as well as rehabilitation services for young girls "at risk" in the United States, while operating private prisons in Europe, Africa, and Australia, also provides equipment and services to Israeli checkpoints in the West Bank along the route of Israel's apartheid wall as well as to the terminals from which Gaza is kept under continuous siege. G4S also provides goods and services to the Israeli police in the West Bank, while it offers security to private businesses and homes in illegal Israeli settlements in occupied Palestine.

As private prison companies have long recognized, the most profitable sector of the prison-industrial complex is immigrant detention and deportation. In the US, G4S provides transportation for deportees who are being ushered out of the US into Mexico, thus colluding with the increasingly repressive immigration practices inside the US. But it was here in the UK where one of the most egregious acts of repression took place in the course of the transportation of an undocumented person.

When I was in London during the month of October, speaking at Birkbeck School of Law, I spoke to Deborah Coles, codirector of the organization Inquest, about the case of Jimmy Mubenga, who died at the hands of G4S guards in the course of a deportation from the UK to Angola. On a British Airways plane, handcuffed behind his back, Mubenga was forcibly pushed by G4S agents against the seat in front of him in the prohibited "carpet karaoke" hold in order to prevent him from vocalizing his resistance. The use of such a term for a law enforcement hold, albeit illegal, is quite astonishing. It indicates that the person subject to the hold is compelled to "sing into the carpet"—or in the case of Mubenga—into the upholstered seat in front, thus rendering his protests muffled and incomprehensible. As Jimmy Mubenga was held for forty minutes, no one intervened. By the time there was finally an attempt to offer him first aid, he was dead.

This appalling treatment of undocumented immigrants from the UK to the US compels us to make connections with Palestinians who have been transformed into immigrants against their will, indeed into undocumented immigrants on their own ancestral lands. I repeat—on their own land. G4S and similar companies provide the technical means of forcibly transforming Palestinian into immigrants on their own land.

As we know, G4S is involved in the operation of private prisons all over the world. The Congress of South African Trade Unions (COSATU) recently spoke out against G4S, which runs the Mangaung Correctional Centre in the Free State. The occasion for their protest was the firing of approximately three hundred members of the police union for staging a strike. According to the COSATU statement:

> G4S's modus operandi is indicative of two of the most worrying aspects of neoliberal capitalism and Israeli apartheid: the ideology of "security" and the increasing privatization of what have been traditionally state run sectors. Security, in this context, does not imply security for everyone, but rather, when one looks at the major clients of G4S Security (banks, governments, corporations etc.) it becomes evident that when G4S says it is "Securing your World," as the company slogan goes, it is referring to a world of exploitation, repression, occupation and racism.

When I traveled to Palestine two years ago with a delegation of indigenous and women-of-color scholar/activists, it was the first time the members of the delegation had actually visited Palestine. Most of us had been involved for many years in Palestine solidarity work, but we were all thoroughly shocked to discover that the repression associated with Israeli settler colonialism was so evident and so blatant. The Israeli military made no attempt to conceal or even mitigate the character of the violence they inflicted on the Palestinian people. Gun-carrying military men and women—many extremely young—were everywhere. The wall, the concrete, the razor wire everywhere conveyed the impression that we were in prison. Before Palestinians are even arrested, they are already in prison. One misstep and one can be arrested and hauled off to prison; one can be transferred from an open-air prison to a closed prison.

G4S clearly represents these carceral trajectories that are so obvious in Palestine but that also increasingly characterize the profit-driven moves of transnational corporations associated with the rise of mass incarceration in the US and the world.

On any given day there are almost 2.5 million people in our country's jails, prisons, and military prisons, as well as in jails in Indian country and immigrant detention centers. It is a daily census, so it doesn't reflect the numbers of people who go through the system every week or every month or every year. The majority are people of color. The fastest-growing sector consists of women—women of color. Many are queer or trans. As a matter of fact, trans people of color constitute the group most likely to be arrested and imprisoned. Racism provides the fuel for maintenance, reproduction, and expansion of the prison-industrial complex.

And so if we say abolish the prison-industrial complex, as we do, we should also say abolish apartheid, and end the occupation of Palestine!

In the United States when we have described the segregation in occupied Palestine that so clearly mirrors the historical apartheid of racism in the southern United States of America—and especially before Black audiences—the response often is: "Why hasn't anyone told us about this before? Why hasn't anyone told us about the segregated highways leading from one settlement to another, about pedestrian segregation regulated by signs in Hebron—not entirely dissimilar from the signs associated with the Jim Crow South. Why hasn't anyone told us this before?"

Just as we say "never again" with respect to the fascism that produced the Holocaust, we should also say "never again" with respect to apartheid in South Africa, and in the southern US. That means, first and foremost, that we will have to expand and deepen our solidarity with the people of Palestine. People of all genders and sexualities. People inside and outside prison walls, inside and outside the apartheid wall.

Boycott G4S! Support BDS!
Palestine will be free!
Thank you.

FIVE

Closures and Continuities

Speech at Birkbeck University (October 25, 2013)

They say that freedom is a constant struggle.
They say that freedom is a constant struggle.
They say that freedom is a constant struggle.
O Lord, we've struggled so long.
We must be free, we must be free.

The title of my talk is drawn from a freedom song that was repeatedly sung in the southern United States during the twentieth-century freedom movement. The other verses of that song evoke crying, sorrow, mourning, dying—*they say freedom is a constant dying / we've died so long we must be free.*

And I like the irony of the last line of each of the verses: *we've struggled so long / we've cried so long / we've sorrowed so long / we've moaned so long / we've died so long / we must be free, we must be free.* And of course there's simultaneously resignation and promise in that line, there is critique and inspiration: *we must be free, we must be free.* But are we really free?

In 2007 I was invited by Baroness Lola Young to speak here in London on the occasion of the bicentennial of the abolition of slavery in the UK. But at the last minute I was unable to make the trip because my mother passed on the day I was scheduled to leave for London. Serendipitously, this is also a year of major anniversaries, anniversaries in the US that reflect the history of the Black freedom struggle. So I've been asked to speak about the meaning of freedom in the sesquicentennial year of the US Emancipation Proclamation and during the fiftieth anniversary year of pivotal events in the twentieth-century Black freedom struggle in the United States.

So let me begin by evoking some of the fiftieth anniversary events. This is the fiftieth anniversary of Dr. Martin Luther King's "Letter from a Birmingham Jail," in which he defended his decision to organize in Birmingham where he was accused of being an outside agitator in this way: "I am cognizant," he wrote, "of the interrelatedness of all communities and states. I cannot sit idly by in Atlanta and not be concerned about what happens in Birmingham. Injustice anywhere is a threat to justice everywhere."

And you are probably familiar with that quote: "We are caught in an inescapable network of mutuality, tied in a single garment of destiny. Whatever affects one directly, affects all indirectly."

And then he proceeds to evoke history: "For more than two centuries," he wrote, "our forebears labored in this country without wages; they made cotton king; they built the homes of their masters while suffering gross injustice and shameful humiliation—and yet out of a bottomless vitality they continued to thrive and develop. If the inexpressible cruelties of slavery could not stop us, the opposition we now face will surely fail."

We're also observing the fiftieth anniversary year of the Birmingham Children's Crusade. It may not be so widely known that the success of the Birmingham campaign was possible because vast numbers of schoolchildren—girls and boys—at the beginning of May, in 1963, faced police dogs and high-power hoses. Their televised demonstrations—and incidentally, television was quite young and it was really the first time that people outside of the South had the opportunity to witness these demonstrations—revealed to the world the determination with which Black people continued to struggle for freedom.

Nineteen sixty-three was also the year of the March on Washington, the March on Washington for Jobs and Freedom, which was attended by some 250,000 people. At that time it was the largest-ever human assembly in Washington.

This past August, there were two marches in Washington, one of which was addressed by Presidents Obama and Clinton, and the other by figures who represent themselves as current civil rights leaders; I won't go into their names.

And there were series of events that marked the fiftieth anniversary. Many people did not know which march to attend (I think one was on the 24th and one was on the 28th). But last month, in September, a number of events took place in Birmingham, Alabama, which as you heard is where I was born and where I grew up.

These events observe the fiftieth anniversary of the bombing of the Sixteenth Street Baptist Church and the killing of four young Black girls. The height of the observances was the bestowal of the highest civilian honor, the Congressional Gold Medal, on the families of the four girls killed in the bombing; although the sister of one of the girls, Sarah Collins (sister of Addie Mae Collins) did not die, she lost an eye and was severely injured and to this day she has received no official assistance with her medical bills.

What I fear about many of these observances is that they tend to enact historical closures. They are represented as historical high points on a road to an ultimately triumphant democracy; one which can be displayed as a model for the world; one which perhaps can serve as justification for military incursions, including the increased use of drones in the so-called war on terror, which has resulted in the killing of vast numbers of people, especially in Pakistan.

While criticizing the Obama administration for the increased use of drones, I must at the same time acknowledge his speech on the fiftieth anniversary of the March on Washington for its attempt to represent freedom struggles as unfinished and for at least attempting to focus on continuities rather than closures. But, invoking the old adage, I must say, that actions really do speak louder than words.

No one can deny that global popular culture is saturated with references to the twentieth-century Black freedom movement. We know that Dr. Martin Luther King Jr. is one of the most widely known historical figures in the world. Inside the US there are more than nine hundred streets named after Dr. King in forty states, Washington, DC, and Puerto Rico. But it has been suggested by geographers who have studied these naming practices that they've been used to deflect attention from persisting social problems—the lack of education, housing, jobs, and the use of carceral strategies to conceal the continued presence of these problems.

There are more than nine hundred streets named after Dr. King, but there are also some 2.5 million people in US jails, prisons, youth facilities, military prisons, and jails in Indian country. The population of those facilities constitute 25 percent of the world's incarcerated population as compared to 5 percent of the planet's population at large. Twenty-five percent of the world's incarcerated population serves as fodder for a vast prison-industrial complex with global dimensions that profits from strategies designed to hide social problems that have remained unaddressed since the era of slavery.

Moreover, police violence and racist vigilante violence is at its height. The Trayvon Martin case in the US recalls the Stephen Lawrence case here. But also Islamophobic violence is nurtured by histories of anti-Black racist violence. There is simultaneously a saturated geographical presence of the culture of the Black freedom movement and a lack of anything more than abstract knowledge about that movement.

I would dare say that most people who are familiar with Dr. Martin Luther King—and the vast majority of people in the world are familiar with him—they know little more than the fact that he had a dream. And of course all of us have had dreams. And as a matter of fact the "I Have a Dream" speech is the most widely circulated of all of his orations.

Relatively few people are aware of the Riverside Church speech on Vietnam and the way he came to recognize the intersections and interconnections of the Black liberation movement and the campaign to end the war in Vietnam. Therefore understandings of the twentieth-century freedom movement that help us cultivate more complicated ideas of the geographies and temporalities of freedom are suppressed.

Dominant representations of the Black freedom movement are a discrete series of historical moments largely produced by the 1955

Montgomery Bus Boycott. And somehow, although Martin Luther King Jr. himself began to emerge to prominence as a consequence of that boycott, he is seen as always already the orator and leader of the civil rights movement.

Even though numbers of books, both scholarly and popular, have been written on the role of women in the 1955 boycott, Dr. King, who was actually invited to be a spokesperson for a movement when he was entirely unknown—the movement had already formed—Dr. King remains the dominant figure.

And I wonder, will we ever truly recognize the collective subject of history that was itself produced by radical organizing? Early on during the 1930s/1940s, and I am referring, for example, to an organization which was known as the Southern Negro Youth Congress, which has largely been excised from the official historical record because some of its key leaders were communists.

As Carole Boyce Davies has pointed out in her wonderful book on Claudia Jones, *Left of Karl Marx*, Claudia Jones was one of the leaders of the Negro Youth Congress (the American Negro Youth Congress and the Southern Youth Congress). And I mention Jones both because of her important work in the US and because she became a pivotal figure in the organizing of Caribbean communities here in Britain after she was arrested for the work she did in the US and eventually deported.

How can we counteract the representation of historical agents as powerful individuals, powerful male individuals, in order to reveal the part played, for example, by Black women domestic workers in the Black freedom movement?

Regimes of racial segregation were not disestablished because of the work of leaders and presidents and legislators, but rather because of the fact that ordinary people adopted a critical stance in the way in which they perceived their relationship to reality. Social realities that may have appeared inalterable, impenetrable, came to be viewed as malleable and transformable; and people learned how to imagine what it might mean to live in a world that was not so exclusively governed by the principle of white supremacy. This collective consciousness emerged within the context of social struggles.

Orlando Patterson has argued that the very concept of freedom—which is held so dear throughout the West, which has inspired so many world historical revolutions—that very concept of freedom must have been first imagined by slaves. During the era of the twentieth-century Black freedom movement, the human beings whose predicament most approximated that of slaves, that of the slaves from whom they were descended, were Black women domestic workers. We're referring to women who cleaned house, who cooked, who were laundrywomen.

As a matter of fact during the 1950s, some 90 percent of all Black women were domestic workers. And given the fact that the majority of people who rode buses in Montgomery, Alabama, in 1955 were Black domestic workers, why is it so difficult to imagine and acknowledge what must have been, among these Black women domestic workers, this amazing collective imagination of a future world without racial and gender and economic oppression?

Even though we may not know the names of all of those women who refused to ride the bus from poor Black communities to affluent white communities in Montgomery, Alabama, it seems that we should at least acknowledge their collective accomplishment. That boycott would not have been successful without their refusals, without their critical refusals. And thus a figure like Dr. Martin Luther King Jr. might never have emerged into prominence.

Fannie Lou Hamer—some of you may have studied the history of the US civil rights movement, the US freedom movement, you may have run across the name of Fannie Lou Hamer—she was a sharecropper and a domestic worker. She was a timekeeper on a cotton plantation in the 1960s. And she emerged as a leader of the Student Nonviolent Coordinating Committee (SNCC) and as a leader of the Mississippi Freedom Democratic Party. She said, "All my life, I have been sick and tired. Now I am sick and tired of being sick and tired."

In 1964, she achieved national prominence when she demanded that members of her Mississippi Freedom Democratic Party, which was a racially integrated party, be seated at the national Democratic Party Convention at the expense of seats that were given to the all-white Democratic Party delegation. In many ways, she paved the way for Barack Obama. But that's another story.

This is not only a year of fiftieth anniversary celebrations, but it is also the sesquicentennial of the Emancipation Proclamation. Interestingly, unfortunately, we have not been called upon to participate in any nationwide anniversary event. I remembered when you here at least had the opportunity to celebrate the bicentennial of the abolition of slavery and, of course, I think your figure is Wilberforce, so you had to also question the fact that a figure like Wilberforce would be symbolic of the abolition of slavery here.

But we haven't even been really asked to participate in any major celebrations. Perhaps the closest we've come to that was the popular film *Lincoln*, which actually focuses on the effort to pass the Thirteenth Amendment. The sesquicentennial of that passage will be coming up in two years. The historical significance of the Emancipation Proclamation is not so much that it enacted the emancipation of people of African descent; on the contrary, it was a military strategy. But if we examine the meaning of this historical moment we might better be able to grasp the failures as well as the successes of emancipation.

I have thought that perhaps we were not asked to reflect on the significance of the Emancipation Proclamation because we might realize that we were never really emancipated. But anyway, at least we might be able to understand the dialectics of emancipation, because we still live with the popular myth that Lincoln freed the slaves and that continues to be perpetuated in popular culture, even by the film *Lincoln*. Lincoln did not free the slaves.

We also live with the myth that the mid-twentieth-century civil rights movement freed the second-class citizens. Civil rights, of course, constitute an essential element of the freedom that was demanded at that time, but it was not the whole story, and maybe we'll get to that later. Eric Foner, in his book called *The Fiery Trial: Abraham Lincoln and American Slavery*, wrote that, and I am quoting:

> The Emancipation Proclamation is perhaps the most misunderstood of the documents that have shaped American history. Contrary to legend, Lincoln did not free the nearly four million slaves with a stroke of his pen. It had no bearing on slaves in the four border states, since they were not in rebellion. The Proclamation also exempted certain parts of the Confederacy occupied by the Union. All told, it left perhaps 750,000 slaves in bondage.

And of course popular narratives about the end of slavery produced by the pronouncing of this emancipation document by

Abraham Lincoln erase the agency of Black people themselves. But, there is something for which Lincoln should be applauded, I believe. And it is that he was shrewd enough to know that the only hope of winning the Civil War resided in creating the opportunity for Black people to fight for their own freedom, and that was the significance of the Emancipation Proclamation.

And as a matter of fact—has that film shown here? Do you remember one of the first scenes, which consists of a conversation with two Black soldiers? I think that perhaps is the most important scene in the film, so people who arrived late missed the most important moment in the film.

And in this connection I'd like to evoke W. E. B. Du Bois and chapter 4 of *Black Reconstruction*, which defined the consequence of the Emancipation Proclamation as a general strike. He uses the vocabulary of the labor movement. And as a matter of fact, chapter 4, "The General Strike," is described in the following manner: "How the Civil War meant emancipation and how the Black worker won the war by a general strike which transferred his labor from the Confederate planter to the Northern invader, in whose army lines workers began to be organized as a new labor force."

And so Du Bois argues that it was the withdrawal and bestowal of labor by slaves that won the war. And what he calls "this army of striking labor" eventually provided the two hundred thousand soldiers, "whose evident ability to fight decided the war." And these soldiers included women like Harriet Tubman, who was a soldier and a spy and had to fight for many years in order to be granted, later, on a soldier's pension.

In the aftermath of the war, we find one of the most hidden eras of US history. And that is the period of Radical Reconstruction.

It certainly remains the most radical era in the entire history of the United States of America. And this is an era that is rarely acknowledged in historical texts. We had Black elected officials, the development of public education. As a matter of fact, former slaves fought for the right to public education; that is to say, education that did not cost money as your education here costs. I'll say parenthetically—the fight was for noncommodified education. And as a matter of fact white children in the South, poor white children who had not had education, gained access to education as a direct result of the struggles of former slaves. There were progressive laws passed challenging male supremacy. This is an era that is rarely acknowledged.

During that era of course we had the creation of what we now call historically Black colleges and universities and there was economic development. This period didn't last very long. From the aftermath of the abolition of slavery, we might take 1865 as that date, until 1877 when Radical Reconstruction was overturned. And it was not only overturned, but it was erased from the historical record. So in the 1960s we confronted issues that should have been resolved in the 1860s, one hundred years later.

As a matter of fact, the Ku Klux Klan and the racial segregation that was so dramatically challenged during the mid-twentieth-century freedom movement was produced not during slavery, but rather in an attempt to manage free Black people who would have otherwise been far more successful in pushing forward democracy for all.

And so we see this dialectical development of the Black liberation movement. There is this freedom movement and then there is an attempt to narrow the freedom movement so that it fits into a much smaller frame, the frame of civil rights. Not that civil rights is not immensely important, but freedom is more expansive than civil rights.

And as that movement grew and developed it was inspired by and in turn inspired liberation struggles in Africa, Asia, Latin America, and Australia. It was not only a question of acquiring the formal rights to fully participate in society, but rather it was also about substantive rights—it was about jobs, free education, free health care, affordable housing, and also about ending the racist police occupation of Black communities.

And so in the 1960s organizations like the Black Panther Party were created. (And I should say the Black Panther Party was founded in 1966, which means that there should be a fiftieth anniversary celebration coming up!) I wonder how we are going to address, for example, the Ten-Point Program of the Black Panther Party. I'll just summarize the Ten-Point Program and you might get an idea why there are not efforts under way to guarantee a large fiftieth anniversary celebration for the Black Panther Party.

Number one was "We want freedom."

Two, full employment.

Three, an end to the robbery by the capitalists of our Black and oppressed communities—it was anticapitalist!

Number four, we want decent housing, fit for the shelter of human beings.

Number five, we want decent education for our people that exposes the true nature of this decadent American society. We want education that teaches us our true history and our role in present-day society.

And number six—which is especially significant in relation to the right-wing effort to undo the very small efforts made by the

Obama administration to produce health care for poor people in the US—we want completely free health care for all Black and oppressed people.

Number seven, we want an immediate end to police brutality and the murder of Black people, other people of color, and all oppressed people inside the United States.

Number eight, we want an immediate end to all wars of aggression—you see how current this still sounds.

Number nine, we want freedom for all Black and oppressed people now held in US federal, state, county, city, and military prisons and jails. We want trials by a jury of peers for all persons charged with so-called crimes under the laws of this country.

And finally, number ten: we want land, bread, housing, education, clothing, justice, peace, and people's community control of modern technology.

What is so interesting about this manifesto is that it recapitulates nineteenth-century abolitionist agendas, and of course the most advanced abolitionists in the nineteenth century recognized that slavery could not be ended by simply negatively abolishing slavery but rather that institutions had to be produced that would incorporate former slaves into a new and developing democracy.

The Black Panther Party was founded in 1966, the program recapitulates abolitionist agendas from the nineteenth century, and it continues to resonate with respect to abolitionist agendas in the twenty-first century.

A member of the Black Panther Party, Herman Wallace, who some of you may be familiar with, he was known as—in circles that continue to engage in campaigns to free political prisoners—as one of the Angola Three. He was released on the first of this month, having spent forty-one years in solitary confinement, and he died on October 4th, three days after being released. If you're interested in Herman Wallace, you might look at the work in which he collaborated, an art piece called *The House That Herman Built*. He was asked by an artist to imagine what kind of house he wanted to live in, and this in the context of having inhabited a six-by-nine-foot cell for almost a half a century.

At the age of sixty-six, another member of the Blank Panther Party, Assata Shakur, who received political asylum in Cuba after escaping from a US prison during the 1980s, was just recently designated one of the Ten Most Wanted terrorists in the world. Assata Shakur, who is a writer and an artist and who had made a life for herself in Cuba, now has to fear Blackwater-type mercenaries who might want to claim the $2 million reward that has been offered in connection with placing her on the Ten Most Wanted terrorist list.

And I should say parenthetically, when I learned about this in May, I remembered when I was placed on the Ten Most Wanted. I didn't make the Ten Most Wanted terrorist list, I think they didn't have one at that time, but I made the Ten Most Wanted criminal list. And I was represented as armed and dangerous. And you know one of the things I remember thinking to myself was, what is this all about? What could I possibly do? And then I realized it wasn't about me at all; it wasn't about the individual at all. It was about sending a message to large numbers of people whom they thought they could discourage from involvement in the freedom struggles at that time.

Assata Shakur is one of the ten most dangerous terrorists in the world according to Homeland Security and the FBI, and then when I think about the violence of my own youth in Birmingham, Alabama, where bombs were planted repeatedly and houses were destroyed and churches were destroyed and lives were destroyed, and we have yet to refer to those acts as the acts of terrorists.

Terrorism, which is represented as external, as outside, is very much a domestic phenomenon. Terrorism very much shaped the history of the United States of America. Acknowledging continuities between nineteenth-century antislavery struggles, twentieth-century civil rights struggles, twenty-first century abolitionist struggles—and when I say abolitionist struggles I'm referring primarily to the abolition of imprisonment as the dominant mode of punishment, the abolition of the prison-industrial complex—acknowledging these continuities requires a challenge to the closures that isolate the freedom movement of the twentieth century from the century preceding and the century following.

It is incumbent upon us not only to recognize these temporal continuities but also to recognize horizontal continuities, links with a whole range of movements and struggles today. And I want very specifically to mention the ongoing sovereignty struggles in Palestine. In Palestine, where not too long ago, Palestinian Freedom Riders set out to contest the apartheid practices of the state of Israel.

But I have been speaking too long. And despite my critique of closures I am compelled by time restrictions to close my talk this evening. So I want to try to close with an opening. All around the world people are saying that we want to struggle together as global communities to create a world free of xenophobia and racism. A world from which poverty has been expunged, and the availability of food is not subject to the demands of capitalist profit. I would say a world where a corporation like Monsanto would be deemed criminal. Where homophobia and transphobia can truly be called historical relics along with the punishment of incarceration and institutions of confinement for disabled people, and where everyone learns how to respect the environment and all of the creatures, human and nonhuman alike, with whom we cohabit our worlds.

SIX

From Michael Brown to Assata Shakur, the Racist State of America Persists

Originally published in the *Guardian*, November 1, 2014

Although racist state violence has been a consistent theme in the history of people of African descent in North America, it has become especially noteworthy during the administration of the first African American president, whose very election was widely interpreted as heralding the advent of a new, postracial era.

The sheer persistence of police killings of Black youth contradicts the assumption that these are isolated aberrations. Trayvon Martin in Florida and Michael Brown in Ferguson, Missouri, are only the most widely known of the countless numbers of Black people killed by police or vigilantes during the Obama administration. And they, in turn, represent an unbroken stream of racist violence, both official and extralegal, from slave patrols and the Ku Klux Klan to contemporary profiling practices and present-day vigilantes.

More than three decades ago Assata Shakur was granted political asylum by Cuba, where she has since lived, studied, and worked as a productive member of society. Assata was falsely charged on numerous occasions in the United States during the early 1970s and vilified by the media. It represented her in sexist terms as "the mother hen" of the Black Liberation Army, which in turn was portrayed as a group with insatiably violent proclivities. Placed on the FBI's Ten Most Wanted list, she was charged with armed robbery, bank robbery, kidnap, murder, and attempted murder of a policeman. Although she faced ten separate legal proceedings, and had already been pronounced guilty by the media, all except one of these trials—the case resulting from her capture—concluded in acquittal, hung jury, or dismissal. Under highly questionable circumstances, she was finally convicted of being an accomplice to the murder of a New Jersey state trooper.

Four decades after the original campaign against her, the FBI decided to demonize her once more. Last year, on the fortieth anniversary of the New Jersey turnpike shootout during which state trooper Werner Foerster was killed, Assata was ceremoniously added to the FBI's Ten Most Wanted terrorists list. To many, this move by the FBI was bizarre and incomprehensible, leading to the obvious question: what interest would the FBI have in designating a sixty-six-year-old Black woman, who has lived quietly in Cuba for the last three and a half decades, as one of the most dangerous terrorists in the world— sharing space on the list with individuals whose alleged actions have provoked military assaults on Iraq, Afghanistan, and Syria?

A partial—perhaps even determining—answer to this question may be discovered in the broadening of the reach of the definition of "terror," spatially as well as temporally. Following the apartheid

South African government's designation of Nelson Mandela and the African National Congress as "terrorists," the term was abundantly applied to US Black liberation activists during the late 1960s and early '70s.

President Nixon's law-and-order rhetoric entailed the labeling of groups such as the Black Panther Party as terrorist, and I myself was similarly identified. But it was not until George W. Bush proclaimed a global war on terror in the aftermath of September 11, 2001, that terrorists came to represent the universal enemy of Western "democracy." To retroactively implicate Assata Shakur in a putative contemporary terrorist conspiracy is also to bring those who have inherited her legacy, and who identify with continued struggles against racism and capitalism, under the canopy of "terrorist violence." Moreover, the historical anticommunism directed at Cuba, where Assata lives, has been dangerously articulated with antiterrorism. The case of the Cuban Five is a prime example of this.

This use of the war on terror as a broad designation of the project of twenty-first-century Western democracy has served as a justification of anti-Muslim racism; it has further legitimized the Israeli occupation of Palestine; it has redefined the repression of immigrants; and has indirectly led to the militarization of local police departments throughout the country. Police departments—including on college and university campuses—have acquired military surplus from the wars in Iraq and Afghanistan through the Department of Defense Excess Property Program. Thus, in response to the recent police killing of Michael Brown, demonstrators challenging racist police violence were confronted by police officers dressed in camouflage uniforms, armed with military weapons, and driving armored vehicles.

The global response to the police killing of a Black teenager in a small Midwestern town suggests a growing consciousness regarding the persistence of US racism at a time when it is supposed to be on the decline. Assata's legacy represents a mandate to broaden and deepen antiracist struggles. In her autobiography published this year, evoking the Black radical tradition of struggle, she asks us to "Carry it on. / Pass it down to the children. / Pass it down. Carry it on . . . / To Freedom!"

SEVEN

The Truth Telling Project: Violence in America

Speech given in St. Louis, Missouri (June 27, 2015)

Kudos to Pastor Cori Bush and Dr. David Ragland for their brilliant work on the Truth Telling Project. I deeply thank you for inviting me to participate in this gathering of Ferguson protesters and other activists in the St. Louis area. It is an honor to join you as you ponder the permanence of violence in America and as you explore old and new meanings and long-standing but unacknowledged truths about the vicious racism that has plagued our world since its beginnings. We know that the historical process of colonization was a violent conquest of human beings and the land they stewarded. It is thus essential that we identify the genocidal assaults on the first peoples of this land as the foundational arena for the many forms of state and vigilante violence that followed. Moreover, the violence of European colonization, including the slave trade, constitutes the common history of Africa, Asia, the Middle East, and the American hemisphere. In other words, there is a longer and larger history of the violence we witness today. Our understandings of and resistance to contemporary modes of racist violence should thus be sufficiently capacious to acknowledge the embeddedness of historical violence—of settler colonial violence against Native Americans and of the violence of slavery inflicted on Africans. Our work today is evidence of the unfinished status of planetary struggles for equality, justice, and freedom.

I thank all of the presenters for their truth-telling presentations, including my sister Fania Davis, who has been working with this project since her first trip to Ferguson. It has been almost one year since the protests last summer following the police killing of Michael Brown. This morning my sister and I touched the ground where he was slain and followed the path of the protesters through the Ferguson community. I know that there are many Ferguson protesters among you and I want you to know how honored I feel to be here in this place at this time. Like everyone else who identifies with current struggles against racism and police violence, I have uttered the words "Ferguson" and "Michael Brown" innumerable times. Both inside and outside the country—for me as for people throughout the world—the very mention of Ferguson evokes struggle, perseverance, courage, and a collective vision of the future.

Let me share a story about the global resonances of your perseverance. Last September when I traveled to Savona, Italy—a town of about sixty thousand people in northwestern Italy near Genoa—where I was invited to speak on the Cuban Five, the people there were eagerly following the Ferguson protests. The group to which I spoke had been working for many years to free the five Cubans who were arrested by the US government in 1998 for attempting to prevent terrorist assaults on Cuba. As you may know, the last three were released this past December in a prisoner exchange. As we gather here this evening, the city of Johannesburg is celebrating the Cuban Five as heroes who represent the collective determination generated by people throughout the world and the uninterrupted sixteen-year-long struggle for their freedom. The point that I want to make is that when I arrived in Savona, the people were also enthusiastically waiting to hear about Michael Brown and Ferguson. They interpreted the actions of the protesters in Ferguson as a blow for freedom all over the planet, including freedom for the Cuban Five.

My primary reason for being here this afternoon is not to offer you leadership or to impart advice as to where to go from here. While I would be happy to engage in such discussions, that is not why I am here. I am here simply because I want to thank you Ferguson activists, because you refused to drop the torch of struggle. When you were urged to go home and go back to business as usual, you said no and in the process you made Ferguson a worldwide symbol of resistance. At a time when we are urged to settle for fast solutions, easy answers, formulaic resolutions, Ferguson protesters said no. You were determined to continue to make the issues of violence against Black communities visible. You refused to believe that there were any simplistic answers and you demonstrated that you would not allow this issue to be buried in the graveyard that has not only claimed Black lives but also so many struggles to defend those lives. So I join the millions of people who thank you for not giving up, for not going home, for staking our claim for freedom on the streets of Ferguson, Missouri, with such great power that Ferguson has become synonymous with progressive protest from Palestine to South Africa, from Syria to Germany, and Brazil to Australia.

I am especially moved to be here where it all began. When Mike Brown was killed almost a year ago, Ferguson activists proclaimed that they were standing up not only for this young man whose life was needlessly sacrificed, but also for countless others. If it had not been for Ferguson, we might not have been compelled to focus our attention on Eric Garner in New York and twelve-year-old Tamir Rice in Cleveland and Walter Scott in North Charleston, South Carolina, and Freddie Gray in Baltimore. If it had not been for Ferguson, we might not have remembered Miriam Carey in Washington, DC, Rekia Boyd in Chicago, and Alesia Thomas in Los Angeles. Had it not been for Ferguson protesters, who also pointed out that Black women and people of color and queer communities and Palestinian activists were targets of officially condoned racist violence, we might not have achieved such a broad consciousness of the work that will be required to build a better world.

We might not have experienced the terrible tragedy in Charleston in ways that have brought together people all over the world, who recognize that racism is indeed alive and well fifteen years into the twenty-first century. We might not have recognized that we have to focus our attention beyond individuals and symbols in order to develop a fluency capable of apprehending the persistence of structural racism even when legalized segregation has been declared historically obsolete, even when individual expressions of racist attitudes are not so easily condoned. Of course it, is a good thing that the Confederate flag is finally on its way out. After more than fifty years of openly symbolizing resistance to civil rights, resistance to Black equality, and anti-Black and anti-Semitic violence, the Confederate flag finally seems to be finally disappearing from our official political landscapes. But the question confronting us is how to identify and challenge structures as well as symbols of racism.

It is quite interesting that in the very last period of Obama's presidency, the Pandora's box of racism has been unbolted. But many are rushing to close it again. In 2011 when Troy Davis faced capital punishment, we desperately tried to build a movement strong enough to save his life. But public understandings of the centrality of the death penalty to the persistence of structural racism were not strong enough to create a collective demand that could not be ignored. In 2012 when Trayvon Martin was killed, the cry "Justice for Trayvon Martin!" awakened people to the urgency of building antiracist movements. But we focused somewhat too sharply on George Zimmerman, the individual perpetrator, to be able to identify the structures of racist violence and specifically the links between vigilante violence and state violence. But when Michael Brown was killed in Ferguson, the movement refused to disband. Even when the police used military technology and tactics to subdue the protesters, they refused to be restrained. Palestinian activists, accustomed to police attacks with tear gas, tweeted advice and encouragement to Ferguson protesters. When some people's rage led them to respond in ways that may have been counterproductive, the movement did not capitulate and refused to disband. Even when people tried to discredit the protesters, the movement refused to disband. When various public figures asked, "Where are the leaders?" the movement said we are not a leaderless movement, we are a leader-*full* movement.

Your movement announced that we do not now need the traditional, recognizable Black male charismatic leader. We definitely love Martin and Malcolm and deeply appreciate their historical contributions, but we need not replicate the past. Besides, this is the twenty-first century and by now we should have learned that leadership is not a male prerogative. Women have always done the work of organizing Black radical movements, so women should also be in the leadership. Within the Black movement, we have engaged in these struggles around gender from the beginning of the twentieth century—and especially in the 1960s and 1970s. Finally we see a movement that values radical Black women, that values radical Black queer women. When Black women stand up—as they did during the Montgomery Bus Boycott—as they did during the Black liberation era, earth-shaking changes occur.

But, as activist historian Barbara Ransby has emphasized, we cannot romanticize leaderlessness. She recently pointed out that:

> Those who romanticize the concept of leaderless movements often misleadingly deploy Ella Baker's words, "Strong people don't need [a] strong leader." Baker delivered this message in various iterations over her fifty-year career working in the trenches of racial-justice struggles, but what she meant was specific and contextual. She was calling for people to disinvest from the notion of the messianic, charismatic leader who promises political salvation in exchange for deference. Baker also did not mean that movements would naturally emerge without collective analysis, serious strategizing, organizing, mobilizing and consensus building.

New organizations such as Black Lives Matter, Dream Defenders, Black Youth Project 100, Justice League NYC, and We Charge Genocide are a few of the new-generation organizations that have developed new models of leadership and that acknowledge how important Black feminist insights are to the development of viable twenty-first-century radical Black movements. These organizations understand the clandestine racialization and gendering of putatively universal categories. They recognize, for example, that those who counter the slogan "Black Lives Matter" with what they assume is a more all-embracing slogan, "All Lives Matter," are often embracing a strategy that glosses over the particular reasons why it is important to insist quite specifically on an end to racist violence. I understand that Hillary Clinton spoke at a church in Florissant, a few days ago, some five miles from Ferguson, where she insisted that "all lives matter." Does she not realize the extent to which such universal proclamations have always bolstered racism? More often than not universal categories have been clandestinely racialized. Any critical engagement with racism requires us to understand the tyranny of the universal. For most of our history the very category "human" has not embraced Black people and people of color. Its abstractness has been colored white and gendered male. I wonder if Hillary Clinton is familiar with the book *All the Women Are White, All the Blacks Are Men, but Some of Us Are Brave.*

If indeed all lives mattered, we would not need to emphatically proclaim that "Black Lives Matter." Or, as we discover on the BLM website: Black Women Matter, Black Girls Matter, Black Gay Lives Matter, Black Bi Lives Matter, Black Boys Matter, Black Queer Lives Matter, Black Men Matter, Black Lesbians Matter, Black Trans Lives Matter, Black Immigrants Matter, Black Incarcerated Lives Matter. Black Differently Abled Lives Matter. Yes, Black Lives Matter, Latino/Asian American/Native American/Muslim/Poor and Working-Class White Peoples Lives matter. There are many more specific instances we would have to name before we can ethically and comfortable claim that All Lives Matter.

In this context I want to take issue with one of Obama's points in his quite amazing eulogy of Reverend Clementa Pinckney in

Charleston, South Carolina, yesterday. I want to take issue with what he said when he exclaimed that if we want to be successful in our struggle against racism we cannot say that we need more conversations about race. Rather we should say that we need action. Certainly we need a great deal more than talk, but it is also the case that we need to learn how to talk about race and racism. If we do not know how to meaningfully talk about racism, our actions will move in misleading directions.

The call for public conversations on race and racism is also a call to develop a vocabulary that permits us to have insightful conversations. If we attempt to use historically obsolete vocabularies, our consciousness of racism will remain shallow and we can be easily urged to assume that, for example, changes in the law spontaneously produce effective changes in the social world. For example, those who assume that because slavery was legally abolished in the nineteenth century, it was thereby relegated to the dustbin of history, fail to recognize the extent to which cultural and structural elements of slavery are still with us. The prison-industrial complex furnishes numerous examples of the persistence of slavery. There are those who believe that we have definitively triumphed in the struggle for civil rights. However, vast numbers of Black people are still deprived of the right to vote—especially if they are in prison or former felons. Moreover, even those who did acquire rights that were not previously available to them did not thereby achieve jobs, education, housing, and health care.

The mid-twentieth-century campaign for civil rights was an essential moment in our struggle for racial equality, but it is important to develop vocabularies that help us acknowledge that civil rights was and is not the entire story. Such an analysis of racism would be helpful to those who are celebrating yesterday's Supreme Court decision on marriage equality as if the final barrier to justice for LGBTQ communities had been surmounted. The decision was indeed historic, but the struggles against homophobic state violence, [for] economic rights, health care, et cetera, continue. Most importantly if the intersectionality of struggles against racism, homophobia, and transphobia is minimized, we will never achieve significant victories in our fight for justice. This is yet another reason why it is essential to develop richer and more critical vocabularies with which to express our insights about racism.

The inability to understand the complexity of racism can lead to assumptions, for example, that there is an independent phenomenon we can call "Black-on-Black crime" that has nothing to do with racism. So, the development of new ways of thinking about racism requires us not only to understand economic, social, and ideological structures, but also collective psychic structures. One of the major examples of the violence of racism consists of the rearing of generations of Black people who have not learned how to imagine the future—who are not now in possession of the education and the imagination that allows them to envision the future. This is violence that leads to other forms of violence—violence against children; violence against partners; violence against friends . . . in our families and communities, we often unconsciously continue the work of larger forces of racism, assuming that this violence is individual and sui generis.

If the popularization of more complex analyses of racism, especially those that have been developed in the context of Black and women-of-color feminisms, can assist us to understand how deeply embedded racist violence [is] in our country's economic and ideological structures, these ways of talking about racism can help us to grasp the global reach of our struggles. Palestinian-Americans' involvement in the Ferguson protests was complemented by expressions of solidarity with Ferguson from Palestinian activists in the West Bank and Gaza. The Ferguson struggle has taught us that local issues have global ramifications. The militarization of the Ferguson police and the advice tweeted by Palestinian activists helped to recognize our political kinship with the boycott, divestment, and sanctions movement and with the larger struggle for justice in Palestine. Moreover, we have come to understand the central role Islamophobia has played in the emergence of new forms of racism in the aftermath of September 11, 2001.

Deep understandings of racist violence arm us against deceptive solutions. When we are told that we simply need better police and better prisons, we counter with what we really need. We need to reimagine security, which will involve the abolition of policing and imprisonment as we know them. We will say demilitarize the police, disarm the police, abolish the institution of the police as we know it, and abolish imprisonment as the dominant mode of punishment. But we will have only just begun to tell the truth about violence in America.

EIGHT

Feminism and Abolition: Theories and Practices for the Twenty-First Century

Speech delivered as the Center for the Study of Race, Politics, and Culture
Annual Public Lecture, in collaboration with the Center for the Study of
Gender and Sexuality at the University of Chicago (May 4, 2013)

Let me say, this is the first time in many years that I have spent an extended period of time in Chicago, that is to say, four days—four whole days. And, if yesterday and today felt like the Chicago I've always known, Tuesday and Wednesday were the most beautiful days in the city I've ever experienced! [*Laughter*] And I started to think, "I can live in Chicago!" until the wind and the cold returned yesterday. But I still like Chicago.

And it is wonderful to be here no matter what the season might be. This amazing city has such a history of struggle. It's the city of the Haymarket Martyrs, the city of radical labor unions, the city of resistance to the police assassinations of Fred Hampton and Mark Clark. It's the city of Puerto Rican activism against colonialism. It's

the city of immigrant rights activists. And of course it is the city of
the Chicago Teachers Union.

Now, a few years ago Chicago was the city that developed a re-
vived national movement to support Assata Shakur, and I remember
Lisa Brock and Derrick Cooper, Tracye Matthews, Beth E. Richie,
Cathy Cohen, and others called for a renewed campaign to defend
the rights and the life of Assata Shakur. Yesterday, May 2, 2013, forty
years after Assata was shot by New Jersey State Police, and falsely
accused of the murder of state trooper Werner Foerster, she became the first woman ever to be placed on the FBI's Most Wanted
terrorists list.

Why, we should ask, was it necessary to put a woman's face on
terrorism, especially in the aftermath of the tragic bombing of the
Boston Marathon? Why was it necessary to put a Black face on terrorism, especially after initial news about the Boston bombing that
the perpetrator was a Black man, or if not a Black man at least a
dark-skinned man in a hoodie—the ghost of Trayvon Martin?

Assata is not a threat in the way she has been represented by the
FBI, as someone who is waiting to commit an act like the Boston
Marathon bombing. Assata is certainly not a terrorist. But if she
would not and is in no position to commit acts of violence against
the US government, the fact that the FBI decided to announce with
great fanfare that she is now the only woman on the Most Wanted
terrorists list should cause us to wonder what the underlying agenda
might be.

And I should say that I especially empathize with Assata, because
it was forty-three years ago that I was placed on the FBI's Ten Most
Wanted list, and, some of you may have seen the new documentary on my trial, which shows President Richard Nixon, openly and

ceremoniously, congratulating the FBI for catching me and in the process labeling me a terrorist as well. So I know the dangerous consequences that can follow from this ideological labeling process.

That this is happening forty years after Assata's original arrest should give us cause to reflect. First of all, it reminds us that there is much work left over from the twentieth century. Especially for those of us who identify as advocates for peace; for racial, gender, sexual justice; for a world that is no longer mutilated by the ravages of capitalism.

We are four decades removed from the era of the 1960s, which is universally remembered as an era for radical and revolutionary activism. Being at a historical distance, however, does not extricate us from the responsibility of defending and indeed liberating those who were and still are willing to give their lives so that we might build a world that is free of racism, and imperialist war, and sexism, and homophobia, and capitalist exploitation.

So I'd like to point out that individual memories are not nearly as long as the memories of institutions, and especially repressive institutions. The FBI is still haunted by the ghost of J. Edgar Hoover. And the CIA and ICE are institutions that have active and vivid memories of the mass organized struggles to end racism, to end war, to overthrow capitalism.

But Leonard Peltier is still behind bars. And Mondo we Langa and Ed Poindexter have been in prison for some forty years. Sundiata Acoli, Assata's comrade, is in prison. Herman Bell, and Veronza Bowers, and Romaine Fitzgerald are still behind bars and my codefendant Ruchell Magee has been in prison for about fifty years, an entire half-century. Two of the Angola Three, Herman Wallace and Albert Woodfox, are still in prison, in solitary confinement. And of course, Mumia Abu-Jamal, although he was released from death row (and that was a people's victory), is still behind bars.

And even as the US government—and this is ironic—singles out Assata as a terrorist, and issues an open invitation to anyone to capture her and bring her back to the US, and there are so many mercenaries, trained by Blackwater and other private security firms, who probably will want to take up that bid for \$2 million. The US government holds in prison within this country five Cubans who attempted to prevent terrorist attacks on Cuba. They were investigating terrorism and in turn were charged with terrorism. I'm referring to the Cuban Five—Free the Cuban Five!

Now, the attack on Assata incorporates the logic of the very terrorism with which they have falsely charged her. What might they expect to accomplish, other than causing new generations of activists to recoil in fear? The FBI is attempting to persuade people, it seems to me, who are the grandchildren of Assata's generation—and mine as well—to turn away from struggles to end police violence, to dismantle the prison-industrial complex, struggles to end violence against women, struggles to end the occupation of Palestine, struggles to defend the rights of immigrants here and abroad.

And I think you here in Chicago should be especially suspicious of the representations of Assata as a cop killer. Her hands were in the air when she was shot in the back, which temporarily paralyzed the arm she would have had to have used to pick up a gun. You should be suspicious, because, according to the Chicago Alliance Against Racist and Political Repression, sixty-three people have been killed by the Chicago Police Department in the last four years. And another 253 have been shot, 172 Black people and twenty-seven Latinos.

You should be *very* suspicious because as more youth are rendered disposable, as more youth become a part of surplus populations that can only be managed through imprisonment, the schools that could begin to solve the problems of disposability are being shut down. According to Karen Lewis, who is one of the most amazing leaders of our time, some sixty-one schools in this city face closure.

And this is a good way to stage our discussion of feminism and abolition, which I consider to be essential theories and practices for the twenty-first century. Assata Shakur, exemplifies within feminist struggles and theories, the way Black women's representations and their involvement in revolutionary struggles militated against prevailing ideological assumptions about women.

In fact, during the latter twentieth century, there were numerous debates about how to define the category "woman." There were numerous struggles over who got included and who was excluded from that category. And these struggles, I think, are key to understanding why there was some measure of resistance from women of color, and also poor and working-class white women, to identify with the emergent feminist movement. Many of us considered that movement at that time to be too white and especially too middle class, too bourgeois.

And in some senses the struggle for women's rights was ideologically defined as a struggle for white middle-class women's rights, pushing out working-class and poor women, pushing out Black women, Latinas, and other women of color from the discursive field covered by the category "woman." The many contestations over this category helped to produce what we came to call "radical women-of-color feminist theories and practices."

At the very time these questions were being raised, these questions about the universality of the category "woman," similar concerns about the category "human" were being debated, especially in
relation to the underlying individualism of human rights discourses.
How could this category be rethought? Not only to embrace Africans, indigenous people, other non-Europeans, but how it might
apply to groups and communities as well, not only to individuals.
And then of course the slogan "Women's Rights Are Human Rights"
began to emerge in the aftermath of an amazing conference that
took place in 1985 in Nairobi, Kenya.

I guess there are some people in the house that attended that
conference, am I right? Okay, I see some hands out there, great. It
was an amazing conference.

At that conference, for the very first time, there was a very large
delegation of US women of color. And I think it was the first time
that US women of color became active in an international arena.
The problem was that many of us then thought that what we needed
to do was to expand the category "women" so that it could embrace Black women, Latina women, Native American women, and
so forth. We thought that by doing that we would have effectively
addressed the problem of the exclusivity of the category. What we
didn't realize then was that we would have to rewrite the whole
category, rather than simply assimilate more women in to an un-
changed category of what counts as "women."

Now a few years earlier, 1979, a white woman by the name of
Sandy Stone was working at the feminist recording company Olivia
Records. Some of you may remember Olivia Records. This woman
was broadly attacked by some self-defined lesbian feminists for not
really being a woman, and for bringing masculine energy into wom-

en's spaces. As it turns out, Sandy Stone was a trans woman, who later wrote some of the germinal texts in the development of transgender studies. This woman was not considered a woman because she was assigned the gender designation of "male" at birth. But this did not prevent her from later asserting a very different gender identity.

So let me fast-forward to the present, when scholars and activists are engaging with questions of prison abolition and gender nonconformity, and have produced some of the most interesting theories, some of the most interesting ideas and approaches to activism.

But before I pursue this line of thought, let me say parenthetically that I had the opportunity this morning to attend a very exciting colloquium on the topic of the asylum and the prison, organized by Professor Bernard Harcourt of the political science department. We can all applaud. And I heard two very brilliant presentations by Michael Rembis and Liat Ben-Moshe. I wish that all of you had been able to hear them. It is often assumed that such issues as psychiatric incarceration and the imprisonment of people who are intellectually and developmentally disabled are marginal questions. However, precisely the opposite turns out to be the case. As both of the presenters emphasized, there is a great deal to be learned about the potential of decarceration and abolition in relation to prisons, about the possibilities of abolishing the prison-industrial complex, by looking very closely at the deinstitutionalization of asylums and psychiatric institutions.

So having said that, what I want to do is address another issue and struggle that is unfortunately too often considered to be marginal to the larger prison abolition struggle.

To return to those historical contestations over the category "woman," let's fast-forward to the present. Let's visit the San Francisco Bay Area where I live, and an organization that is called

Transgender, Gender Variant, Intersex Justice Project. Now, TGI Justice Project is an organization led by women of color, by trans women of color. The executive director is a woman whose name is Miss Major. And, yeah, I'll tell Miss Major that she got a lot of applause in Chicago, and that's especially important because she was raised on the South Side of Chicago, not very far from here. She describes herself as a Black, formerly incarcerated, male-to-female transgender elder, born and raised on the South Side of Chicago, and a veteran activist. She participated in the Stonewall Rebellion in 1969. But she said she was not really politicized until the wake of the Attica Prison Rebellion. I was just talking to her the other day and learned that the person who politicized her is Big Black, one of the Attica defendants and a close friend of mine until his death. Frank Smith was known as Big Black, one of the leaders of the Attica Rebellion, who eventually won a lawsuit against the state of New York in connection with Attica. Miss Major met him in prison. She said that he was not only totally accepting of her gender presentation, but he instructed her on so many issues regarding the relationship between racism, and imperialism, and capitalism.

Now, TGI Justice Project is a grassroots organization that advocates for, defends, and includes primarily trans women and trans women of color. These are women who have to fight to be included within the category "woman" in a way that is not dissimilar from the earlier struggles of Black women and women of color who were assigned the gender female at birth. Moreover, they have worked out what I see as a deeply feminist approach that we would do well to understand and emulate.

Miss Major says she prefers to be called Miss Major, not Ms. Major, because as a trans woman she is not yet liberated. The work

of TGIJP is deeply feminist because it is performed at the intersection of race, class, sexuality, and gender, and because it moves from
addressing the individual predicaments of the members of their
community, who constitute the individuals who are *most* harassed
by law enforcement, *most* arrested and incarcerated, to larger questions of the prison industrial complex. Trans women of color end
up primarily in male prisons—especially if they have not undergone gender reassignment surgery, and many of them don't want to
undergo that surgery. And sometimes even if they have undergone
the surgery, they end up being placed in men's prisons. After they
are imprisoned they often receive more violent treatment by the
guards than anyone else, and on top of that, they are marked by the
institution as targets of male violence. This is so much the case that
cops so easily joke about the sexual fate of trans women in the male
prisons where they are usually sent. Male prisons are represented
as violent places. But we see, especially by looking at the predicament of trans women, that this violence is often encouraged by the
institutions themselves.

Many of you are familiar with the Minneapolis case of CeCe
McDonald, who was charged with murder after an encounter with
a group that yelled out racist, homophobic, and transphobic slurs all
at the same time. She is now in a men's prison in Minnesota, serving a three-and-a-half-year sentence. But on top of this violence, trans
women are often denied their hormonal treatments, even if they
have valid prescriptions.

The point that I'm trying to make is that we learn a great deal
about the reach of the prison system, about the nature of the prison-industrial complex, about the reach of abolition by examining the
particular struggles of trans prisoners, and especially trans women.

Perhaps most important of all, and this is so central to the development of feminist abolitionist theories and practices: we have to learn how to think and act and struggle against that which is ideologically constituted as "normal." Prisons are constituted as "normal." It takes a lot of work to persuade people to think beyond the bars, and to be able to imagine a world without prisons and to struggle for the abolition of imprisonment as the dominant mode of punishment.

And we can ask ourselves in that context, why are trans women—and especially Black trans women who cannot easily pass—why are they considered so far outside the norm? They are considered outside the norm by almost everyone in the society.

And of course we've learned a great deal about gender over the past decades. I suppose just about everyone who's in the field of feminist studies has read Judith Butler's *Gender Trouble*. But you should also read Beth Richie's most recent book, an amazing book called *Arrested Justice: Black Women, Violence and America's Prison Nation*. And specifically look at her account of the case of the New Jersey Four, of four young Black lesbians who were just walking around having fun in Greenwich Village, but ended up in prison because they defended themselves from male violence. This violence was further consolidated by the fact that they saw themselves represented in the media as "a lesbian wolf pack." We see that here race, gender, sexual nonconformity can lead to racist bestialization! Which is an attack, as one of my students, Eric Stanley, points out in his dissertation, not only against the humans but against the animals as well.

TGI Justice Project is an abolitionist organization. It calls for a dialectic of service provision and abolitionist advocacy. TGIJP thus promotes a kind of feminism that urges us to be flexible, one that warns us not to become too attached to our objects, whether they are objects of study—I say that for the academics in the house—or whether they are objects of our organizing—I say this for the activists in the house.

TGI Justice Project shows us that these objects can become something entirely different as a result of our work. It shows us that the process of trying to assimilate into an existing category in many ways runs counter to efforts to produce radical or revolutionary results. And it shows us that we not only should not try to assimilate trans women into a category that remains the same, but that the category itself has to change so it does not simply reflect normative ideas of who counts as women and who doesn't.

But by extension, there's another lesson: don't even become too attached to the concept of gender. Because, as a matter of fact, the more closely we examine it, the more we discover that it is embedded in a range of social, political, cultural, and ideological formations. It is not one thing. There is not one definition, and certainly gender cannot now be adequately described as a binary structure with "male" being one pole and "female" at the other.

And so, bringing trans women, trans men, intersex, many other forms of gender nonconformity into the concept of gender, it radically undermines the normative assumptions of the very concept of gender.

I want to share with you this wonderful quote from Dean Spade, who I understand spoke yesterday: "From my understanding," he writes,

> a central endeavor of feminist, queer, and trans activists has been to dismantle the cultural ideologies, social practices, and legal norms that say certain body parts determine gender identity and gendered social characteristics and roles. We have fought against

the idea that the presence of uteruses, or ovaries, or penises, or testicles, should be understood to determine such things as people's intelligence, proper parental roles, proper physical appearance, proper gender identity, proper labor roles, proper sexual partners and activities, and capacity to make decisions. We have opposed medical and scientific assertions that affirm the purported health of traditional gender roles and activities that pathologize bodies that defy these norms. We continue to work to dispel myths that body parts somehow make us who we are (and make us "less than" or "better than," depending on which we may have).

Trans scholar-activists are doing some of the most interesting work on prison abolition. So I want to mention three recent books by scholar-activists who engage with trans abolitionist politics. And, one of them is a wonderful anthology edited by Eric Stanley and Nat Smith called *Captive Genders: Trans Embodiment and the Prison Industrial Complex*. Andrea Ritchie, Kay Whitlock, and Joey Mogul just recently published an anthology called *Queer (In)Justice: The Criminalization of LGBT People in the United States*. And Dean Spade, who I quoted—he's so amazingly prolific, I can't imagine how he writes all of these books and articles, and he's always on the front line in demonstrations all over the world—recently published a book entitled *Normal Life: Administrative Violence, Critical Trans Politics, and the Limits of Law*.

All three of these texts are feminist, not so much because they address a feminist object—although racism, the prison-industrial complex, criminalization, captivity, violence, and the law are all objects that feminism should analyze, criticize, and also resist through struggle—but I see these texts as feminist primarily because of their methodologies. And feminist methodologies can assist us all in major ways as researchers, academics, and as activists and organizers.

When we discover what appears to be one relatively small and marginal aspect of the category—or what is struggling to enter the category, so that it can basically bust up the category—this process can illuminate so much more than simply looking at the normative dimensions of the category. And, you know, academics are trained to fear the unexpected, but also activists always want to have a very clear idea of our trajectories and our goals. And in both instances we want *control*. We want control, so that oftentimes our scholarly and activist projects are formulated just so that they reconfirm what we already know. But that is not interesting. It is boring. And so how to allow for surprises, and how do we make these surprises productive?

Let me just make a tangential remark here, because in many ways this is about how to build on the surprise element. When I was in high school I really loved to square dance. [*Laughs*] I did, I loved it! And later on, toward the time of the Black liberation movement, somebody told me that "Black people don't square dance! Why are you square dancing, Black people don't square dance!" And most recently of course I came across the Carolina Chocolate Drops, who are absolutely incredible. But I also ran across the story that I want to share with you about a square dance caller here in Chicago. And, I think her name is Saundra Bryant, I read this somewhere online. The square dance caller said she received a telephone call from someone who wanted her to call for their square dance club. And so she says, "Okay, let me look at my calendar," but then the person quickly interjected, "Before you look at your calendar, you should know that we are a gay square dance club." And so she quickly retorted, "Well, before I look at my calendar, you should know that

I am a Black square dance caller." So at that moment square dancing became both Black and gay, which probably changed something
about square dancing as well.

You may think I was digressing, but not really, because I want to
emphasize the importance of approaching both our theoretical explo-
rations and our movement activism in ways that enlarge and expand
and complicate and deepen our theories and practices of freedom.

Feminism involves so much more than gender equality. And it
involves so much more than gender. Feminism must involve a consciousness of capitalism—I mean, the feminism that I relate to. And
there are multiple feminisms, right? It has to involve a consciousness
of capitalism, and racism, and colonialism, and postcolonialities, and
ability, and more genders than we can even imagine, and more sexualities than we ever thought we could name. Feminism has helped
us not only to recognize a range of connections among discourses,
and institutions, and identities, and ideologies that we often tend to
consider separately. But it has also helped us to develop epistemological and organizing strategies that take us beyond the categories
"women" and "gender." And, feminist methodologies impel us to explore connections that are not always apparent. And they drive us to
inhabit contradictions and discover what is productive in these contradictions. Feminism insists on methods of thought and action that
urge us to think about things together that appear to be separate,
and to disaggregate things that appear to naturally belong together.

Now, the assumption has been that because transgender and
gender-nonconforming populations are relatively small (for example, within a prison system that in the US constitutes almost 2.5
million people and more than 8 million people in jails and prisons
worldwide), therefore, why should they deserve very much atten-

tion? But feminist approaches to the understanding of prisons, and indeed the prison-industrial complex, have always insisted that, for example, if we look at imprisoned women, who are also a very small percentage throughout the world, we learn not only about women in prison, but we learn much more about the system as a whole than we would learn if we look exclusively at men. Thus, also, a feminist approach would insist both on what we can learn from, and what we can transform, with respect to trans and gender-nonconforming prisoners, but also it insists on what this knowledge and activism tells us about the nature of punishment writ large—about the very apparatus of prison.

It is true that we cannot begin to think about the abolition of prisons outside of an antiracist context. It is also true that antiprison abolition embraces or should embrace the abolition of gender policing. That very process reveals the epistemic violence—and the feminist studies students in here know what I'm talking about—the epistemic violence that is inherent in the gender binary in the larger society.

So bringing feminism within an abolitionist frame, and vice versa, bringing abolition within a feminist frame, means that we take seriously the old feminist adage that "the personal is political." The personal is political—everybody remembers that, right? The personal is political. We can follow the lead of Beth Richie in thinking about the dangerous ways in which the institutional violence of the prison complements and extends the intimate violence of the family, the individual violence of battery and sexual assault. We also question whether incarcerating individual perpetrators does anything more than reproduce the very violence that the perpetrators have allegedly committed. In other words criminalization allows the problem to persist.

And it seems to me that people who are working on the front line of the struggle against violence against women should also be on the front line of abolitionist struggles. And people opposed to police crimes, should also be opposed to domestic—what is constructed as domestic—violence. We should understand the connections between public violence and private or privatized violence.

There is a feminist philosophical dimension of abolitionist theories and practices. The personal is political. There is a deep relationality that links struggles against institutions and struggles to reinvent our personal lives, and recraft ourselves. We know, for example, that we replicate the structures of retributive justice oftentimes in our own emotional responses. Someone attacks us, verbally or otherwise, our response is what? A counterattack. The retributive impulses of the state are inscribed in our very emotional responses. The political reproduces itself through the personal. This is a feminist insight—a Marxist-inflected feminist insight—that perhaps reveals some influence of Foucault. This is a feminist insight regarding the reproduction of the relations that enable something like the prison-industrial complex.

The imprisoned population could not have grown to almost 2.5 million people in this country without our implicit assent. And we don't even acknowledge the fact that psychiatric institutions are often an important part of the prison-industrial complex, nor do we acknowledge the intersection of the pharmaceutical-industrial complex and the prison-industrial complex.

But the point I make is that if we had mounted a more powerful resistance in the 1980s and 1990s during the Reagan-Bush era and during the Clinton era, we would not be confronting such a behemoth today.

We have had to unlearn a great deal over the course of the last few decades. We have had to try to unlearn racism, and I am speaking not only about white people. People of color have had to unlearn the assumption that racism is individual, that it is primarily a question of individual attitudes that can be dealt with through sensitivity training.

You remember that Don Imus called the Rutgers women's basketball team "nappy-headed hoes" about five years ago? Five years later he's rehabilitated! But of course this doesn't compensate for the fact that Troy Davis is dead, his life claimed by the most racist of all of our institutions, capital punishment. No amount of psychological therapy or group training can effectively address racism in this country, unless we also begin to dismantle the structures of racism.

Prisons are racism incarnate. As Michelle Alexander points out, they constitute the new Jim Crow. But also much more, as the lynchpins of the prison-industrial complex, they represent the increasing profitability of punishment. They represent the increasingly global strategy of dealing with populations of people of color and immigrant populations from the countries of the Global South as surplus populations, as disposable populations.

Put them all in a vast garbage bin, add some sophisticated electronic technology to control them, and let them languish there. And in the meantime, create the ideological illusion that the surrounding society is safer and more free because the dangerous Black people and Latinos, and the Native Americans, and the dangerous Asians and the dangerous White people, and of course the dangerous Muslims, are locked up!

And in the meantime, corporations profit and poor communities suffer! Public education suffers! Public education suffers because it is not profitable according to corporate measures. Public health care suffers. If punishment can be profitable, then certainly health care should be profitable, too. This is absolutely outrageous! It is outrageous.

It is also outrageous that the state of Israel uses the carceral technologies developed in relation to US prisons not only to control the more than eight thousand Palestinian political prisoners in Israel but also to control the broader Palestinian population.

These carceral technologies, for example, the separation wall, which reminds us of the US-Mexico border wall, and other carceral technologies are the material constructs of Israeli apartheid.

G4S, the organization, the corporation G4S, which profits from the incarceration and the torturing of Palestinian prisoners, has a subsidiary called G4S Secure Solutions, which was formerly known as Wackenhut. And just recently a subsidiary of *that* corporation, GEO Group, which is a private prison company, attempted to claim naming rights at Florida Atlantic University by donating something like $6 million, right? And, the students rose up. They said that our football stadium will not bear the name of a private prison corporation! And the students won. The students won; the name came down from the marquee.

From California or Texas or Illinois to Israel and Occupied Palestine, and then back to Florida, we should not have allowed this to happen. We should not have allowed this to happen over the last three decades. And we cannot allow it to continue today.

And let me say that I really love the new generations of young students and workers. Two generations removed from my own; they say sometimes revolution skips a generation. But that skipped generation has also worked hard! Those of you who are in your forties, if you hadn't done the work that you did, then it would not be possible for the younger generation to emerge. And what I like most about the younger generation is that they are truly informed by feminism. Even if they don't know it, or even if they don't admit it! They are informed by antiracist struggles. They are not infected with the emotionally damaging homophobia which has been with us for so long. And they are taking the lead in challenging transphobia along with racism and Islamophobia. So I like working with young people because they allow me to imagine what it is like not to be so totally overburdened with decades of oppressive ideology.

Now, I just have a couple of more things to say. I know I'm over my time and I apologize. But I just have one more page of notes. [*Laughter*]

And so let me say that marriage equality is more and more acceptable precisely because of young people. But, many of these young people also remind us that we have to challenge the assimilationist logic of the struggle for marriage equality! We cannot assume that once outsiders are allowed to move into the circle of the bourgeois hetero-patriarchal institution of marriage, the struggle has been won.

Now, the story of the interrelationships between feminism and abolitionism has no appropriate end. And with this conversation we have just begun to explore a few of its dimensions. But if I have not come to the end of the story, I have certainly come to the end of my time. So I want to let Assata Shakur have the last word tonight. "At this moment," she wrote a few years ago,

> I am not so concerned about myself. Everybody has to die sometime, and all I want is to go with dignity. I am more concerned

about the growing poverty, the growing despair that is rife in America. I am more concerned about our younger generations, who represent our future. I am more concerned about the rise of the prison-industrial complex that is turning our people into slaves again. I am more concerned about the repression, the police brutality, violence, the rising wave of racism that makes up the political landscape of the US today. Our young people deserve a future, and I consider it the mandate of my ancestors to be a part of the struggle to ensure that they have one.

NINE

Political Activism and Protest from the 1960s to the Age of Obama

Speech at Davidson College (February 12, 2013)

Thank you so much and good evening everyone. First of all it is a pleasure and an honor to be here at Davidson College to help you celebrate Black History Month. I always welcome the opportunity to come to North Carolina because I spent a number of years of my own activist career doing work in this state.

So first of all, let me say that Black History Month falls in the month of February, about which people used to complain because it's the shortest month of the year, but there are specific reasons, including the birthday of Frederick Douglass, why we observe Black history during this month. And I should also say that since we began to celebrate the birthday of Dr. Martin Luther King in the middle of January we've extended our February celebration so now at least we have a month and a half. And those of us who recognize the constitutive role that Black women have played in the struggle for women's rights in this country continue to celebrate Black history during Women's History Month, which means that we now have two and a half months to specifically recognize Black history. That's not that bad.

Black history, whether here in North America, or in Africa, or in Europe, has always been infused with a spirit of resistance, an activist spirit of protest and transformation. So I'm happy to be invited to address the topic of social protest and transformation from the sixties to the present.

When we celebrate Black history it is not primarily for the purpose of representing individual Black people in the numerous roles as first to break down barriers in the many fields that have been historically closed to people of color, although it is extremely important to acknowledge these firsts. But rather, we celebrate Black history, I believe, because it is a centuries-old struggle to achieve and expand freedom for us all. And so Black history is indeed American history, but it is also world history. There is a reason why in 2008 there was such a planetary euphoria when Obama was elected. That a Black man who identified with the spirit of the historical struggle for Black liberation could be elected president of the United States was a cause for rejoicing everywhere in the world, because people everywhere have identified with this sustained struggle for freedom or what Cedric Robinson calls "the Black radical tradition."

It is a tradition that can be claimed by people everywhere. Regardless of race, regardless of nationality, regardless of geographical location. Moreover, Black Americans have been the beneficiaries of solidarity generated in all parts of the world. Frederick Douglass traveled to Europe to gain support for antislavery abolition. Ida B. Wells traveled to England and Ireland and Scotland to generate support for the antilynching movement. And then of course Canada offered sanctuary from slavery. When the Fugitive Slave Law prevented those who escaped from slavery from finding refuge anywhere inside the United States, the Underground Railroad had to extend up to Canada.

And then of course we can talk about cases such as the Scottsboro Nine. My mother was one of the many activists who joined the struggle to free the Scottsboro Nine in the 1930s and the 1940s. An international campaign developed, although it would be many decades before the last of the Scottsboro Nine were freed. In the 1950s there was a notorious case in North Carolina known as the Kissing Case. In Monroe, North Carolina, in 1958, a young Black boy about six years old kissed a white girl with whom he was playing and was arrested on attempted rape charges. I mention this case not so much because of its spectacular character, but because of the media attention generated in Europe that eventually led to the freeing of this young boy. And then of course there are numerous political prisoners who have been the beneficiaries of global solidarity movements. I include myself among those political prisoners.

When I was in jail there were campaigns literally all over the world. In Asia, in Africa, in Latin America, in Europe, in the former Soviet Union, in Germany—both East and West. You heard from Professor Caplan . . . about the current case of Mumia Abu-Jamal, whose plight is the subject of more public discussion in Europe than here in the United States. And then of course the founding of the Black Panther Party not only captured the imagination of young people all over the United States within a very short period of time; there were Black Panther Party chapters in every major city in this country. And you'll have the opportunity to hear from the head of

the Black Panther Party in Winston-Salem, next Monday I believe.
But Black Panther Parties were created in places like New Zealand.
Maori people who were struggling against racism in New Zealand
created a Black Panther Party. In Brazil there was a Black Panther
Party. In Israel there was a Black Panther Party.

So I want us to think about the very capacious framework within
which the protests and struggles for Black liberation evolved. People
all over the world have been inspired by the Black freedom movement to forge activist movements addressing oppressive conditions
in their own countries. In fact you might say that there has been
a symbiotic relationship between struggles abroad and struggles
at home, relationships of inspiration and mutuality. The historical
South African freedom struggle was inspired in part by the historical Black American freedom struggle. The Black American freedom
struggle was inspired in part by the South African freedom struggle.
In fact, I can remember growing up in the most segregated city in
the country, Birmingham, Alabama, and learning about South Africa
because Birmingham was known as the Johannesburg of the South.
Dr. Martin Luther King was inspired by Gandhi to engage in nonviolent campaigns against racism. And in India, the Dalits, formerly
known as untouchables and other people who've been struggling
against the caste system have been inspired by the struggles of Black
Americans. More recently, young Palestinians have organized Freedom Rides, recapitulating the Freedom Rides of the 1960s by board-
ing segregated buses in the occupied territory of Palestine and being
arrested as the Black and white Freedom Riders were in the sixties.
They announced their project to be the Palestinian Freedom Riders.

So I want us to think about this more capacious framework
within which to consider Black history. I want to express concern

that our collective relationship to history in this country is seriously flawed. Of course many of you are familiar with the William Faulkner quote that bears repeating: "The past is never dead. The past is never dead. It's not even past." And so we live with the ghosts of our past. We live with the ghosts of slavery. And I wonder why in 2013 we are not vigorously celebrating the 150th anniversary of the Emancipation Proclamation. Do you find that strange? I know that Obama issued a proclamation on December 31 urging people to celebrate the anniversary of the Emancipation Proclamation, but I don't know anyone who did. Do you? Then I'm also wondering what will be on the agenda for the 150th anniversary of the passage of the Thirteenth Amendment. Maybe another film?

So I want to pursue this theme of living with the ghosts of our pasts. I've been asked to talk about the protest movements of the sixties. But those protest movements would not have been necessary—it would not have been necessary to create a mid-century Black freedom movement had slavery been comprehensively abolished in the nineteenth century. The movement we call the "civil rights movement," and that was called by most of its participants the "freedom movement," reveals an interesting slippage between freedom and civil rights, as if civil rights has colonized the whole space of freedom, that the only way to be free is to acquire civil rights within the existing framework of society. Had slavery been abolished in 1863, through the Emancipation Proclamation, or in 1865 through the Thirteenth Amendment, Black people would have enjoyed full and equal citizenship and it would not have been necessary to create a new movement.

One of the most hidden eras of US history is the period of Radical Reconstruction. It was certainly the most radical period.

There were Black elected officials. Then we had to wait more than another century to get them back. There was the development of public education. People in this country are still unaware of the fact that former slaves brought public education to the South. That white kids in the South would never have had the opportunity to get an education had not it been for the persistent campaigns for education. Because education was equivalent to liberation. No liberation without education. And then of course there was the economic development during that brief period. I'm talking about the period between 1865 and 1877, Radical Reconstruction. As a matter of fact, many progressive laws were passed when Black people were in the legislatures of various states, progressive laws with respect to women's rights as well, not just with respect to issues of race.

I've been thinking that if we really manage to celebrate the 150th anniversary of the Emancipation Proclamation and we have another couple of years between now and the sesquicentennial of the Thirteenth Amendment, every person in this country, from high school to the postgraduate level, should read W. E. B. Du Bois's *Black Reconstruction in America*. In the 1960s we confronted issues that should have been resolved in the 1860s. And I'm making this point because what happens when 2060 rolls around? Will people still be addressing these same issues? And I also think it's important for us to think forward and to imagine future history in a way that is not restrained by our own lifetimes. Oftentimes people say, well, if it takes that long, I'll be dead. So what? Everybody dies, right? And if people who were involved in the struggle against slavery—I'm thinking about people like Frederick Douglass, or Ida B. Wells in the struggle against lynching—if they had that very narrow individualistic sense of their own contributions, where would we be today? And so we have to learn how to imagine the future in terms that are not restricted to our own lifetimes.

One of the things I did in North Carolina in the seventies was to battle with the Klan because the Ku Klux Klan really controlled this state. I was telling some people during dinner that I can remember when there were big billboards of the Knights of the Ku Klux Klan welcoming visitors to the various cities and towns of North Carolina. And members of the Klan appeared publicly in their garb. As I told people at dinner, I helped to organize two major marches in Raleigh, North Carolina, through my involvement in a multiracial organization, the National Alliance Against Racist and Political Repression. We had some of our white members hang out at the Klan bars in order to gather intelligence about what the Klan was planning. We were actually very frightened that they might—given the history of the Klan committing violence against Black people, not only in the past, but then in the sixties and the seventies—we were afraid that they might be targeting us.

When we speak about the Klan as symbolic of the whole edifice of racism, when we think about racial segregation, we often assume that it originated in slavery. But the Ku Klux Klan was founded in the aftermath of slavery, right? Racial segregation was instituted in the aftermath of slavery, in the aftermath of Black Radical Reconstruction, in an attempt to manage free Black people. What did it mean during those days for people who had been historically subjugated and kept in chains to have the opportunity to express themselves freely? Well, there were those who did not want to see this. Of course there were those who wanted to bring slavery back into the picture. But there were many strategies that were used to manage free Black bodies.

Had those strategies not been implemented, such as the violence associated with the Ku Klux Klan, such as the convict lease system, which created the basis for the punishment industry today, had that not happened free Black people would have been far more successful in pushing for democracy for all people in this country. The struggles of the 1960s would have been unnecessary if Black people had acquired full citizenship in the aftermath of slavery. But when we focus our attention on the southern struggles of the 1950s and '60s, specifically when we think about the Montgomery Bus Boycott, we inevitably evoke Dr. Martin Luther King. We also think about Rosa Parks, but we should be focusing on Jo Ann Robinson as well, who wrote the book *The Montgomery Bus Boycott and the Women Who Started It*. As many times as I've spoken during Black History Month, I never tire of urging people to remember that it wasn't a single individual or two who created that movement, that, as a matter of fact, it was largely women within collective contexts, Black women, poor Black women who were maids, washerwomen, and cooks. These were the people who collectively refused to ride the bus.

These are the people whom we have to thank for imagining a different universe and making it possible for us to inhabit this present. There was Claudette Colvin, too, who has a wonderful book, *Twice Toward Justice*. All of you should read it because Claudette Colvin refused to move to the back of the bus before Rosa Parks's action. Claudette Colvin was also arrested before. You see, we think individualistically, and we assume that only heroic individuals can make history. That is why we like to focus on Dr. Martin Luther King, who was a great man, but in my opinion his greatness resided precisely in the fact that he learned from a collective movement. He transformed in his relationship with that movement. He did not see himself as a single individual who was going to bring freedom to the oppressed masses.

Then of course there was the bombing of the Sixteenth Street Baptist Church. I think that the larger symbolic meaning of the deaths of Carole Robertson, Cynthia Wesley, Addie Mae Collins, and Denise McNair, who were killed that Sunday morning in Birmingham, Alabama, has to do with the snuffing out of the lives of Black girls, who thus never had an opportunity to grow into women committed to the struggle for freedom. And it's interesting because some months before they were killed, there were the children's marches. During the children's marches in Birmingham, children who stood up to the police, who stood up to the firemen with their high-power water hoses, and their dogs were responsible for some of the most dramatic moments of the entire campaign. Children were committed to justice. All of this gets erased when you obsessively focus on single individuals.

So let me return again to this theme of the Black freedom movement, the civil rights movement. The freedom movement was expansive. It was about transforming the entire country. It was not simply about acquiring civil rights within a framework that itself would not change. There has been an attempt to co-opt that movement for purposes of creating a historical memory that fits into the smaller frame of civil rights. And I'm not suggesting of course that civil rights are not important. There are still many significant civil rights movements in the twenty-first century. The struggle for immigrant rights is a civil rights struggle. The struggle to defend the rights of prisoners is a civil rights struggle. The struggle for marriage equality with respect to LGBT communities is a civil rights struggle. But freedom is still more expansive than civil rights. And in the sixties there were some of us who insisted that it was not simply a question of acquiring the formal rights to fully participate in a society, but rather it was also about the forty acres and the mule that was dropped from the abolitionist agenda in the nineteenth century. It was about economic freedom.

It was about substantive freedoms. It was about free education. It was about free health care. Affordable housing. These are issues that should have been on the abolitionist agenda in the nineteenth century, and here we are in the twenty-first century and we still can't say that we have affordable housing and health care, and education has thoroughly become a commodity. It has been so thoroughly commoditized that many people don't even know how to understand the very process of acquiring knowledge because it is subordinated to the future capacity to make money. So it was about free education and free health care and affordable housing. It was about ending the racist police occupation of Black communities. These were some of the demands raised by the Black Panther Party.

I live in Oakland, California, the city where the Black Panther Party was created in 1966. We still have major issues with police racism, police violence. I spoke not long ago at an event in celebration of the seventeenth birthday of a young man who had been recently killed near one of the high schools by the police. Then, let's remember that Trayvon Martin would have also been eighteen, right? How many of you are familiar with the Ten-Point Program of the Black Panther Party?

I find it so interesting that certain moments in the history of the Black freedom struggle can be very easily incorporated into a larger narrative of the struggle for democracy in this country, and then there are others that get completely ignored. I don't think that there is a single person in this country who doesn't know the name of Dr. Martin Luther King, probably very few people in the world who don't know his name and that's wonderful. Let me add that the new monument in Washington is really quite striking. I understand that they are going to remove the misquoted phrase that says, "I was a drum major for justice, peace and righteousness." MLK actually said, "If you want to say that I was a drum major, say that I was a drum major for peace. Say that I was a drum major for justice, a drum major for righteousness." Yet the monument is actually quite striking. On this Martin Luther King Day, the day of Obama's second inauguration, I happened to be in Washington, DC, attending the Peace Inaugural Ball organized by Andy Shallal with Mos Def and Sweet Honey in the Rock. When the ball was over a small group of us decided to visit the monument. I didn't realize I would be so moved by this monument, but it was quite amazing to witness it at two thirty in the morning, when no one else was there. We were able to walk along the wall and read the various quotations inscribed in the wall. It made me feel that we have indeed come a long way, but at the same time we have regressed so much. So how do you address that contradiction of progress and regression at the very same time? I mention this because there's a reason why most people never have the opportunity to look at the Black Panther Party "Ten-Point Program," because those points are still very much on the agenda today. Those aspects of the struggle that are incorporated into the official narrative of American democracy are aspects that can be considered to have achieved their own closure. So Black people have civil rights. It's no longer necessary to struggle for civil rights. Thus the struggle for freedom can be relegated to the past. But of course, this is true.

I was originally planning to read the ten points, but I think I will ask you to Google "Ten-Point Program Black Panther Party" and you'll see among the ten points, "We want completely free health care for all Black and oppressed people." Read this point now at a time when people are troubled about the health care program that Obama supported, which is better than nothing I suppose . . . but not too much better than nothing. You will also find the point that says, "We want freedom for all Black and oppressed people now held in US federal, state, county, city and military prisons and jails." Now that we know that there are 2.5 million people behind bars, as Professor Caplan pointed out, and that, according to Michelle Alexander, there are more Black people incarcerated and directly under the control of correctional agencies in the second decade of the twenty-first century than there were enslaved in 1850.

◆

Social protests from the sixties to the present . . . if we have a hard time grappling with history or acknowledging how we inhabit our histories, this trouble with history can also be seen in the way in which our current mass actions are often subjected to a media process, a mediated process of becoming stale news. So that something that happened as recently as a year ago—the Occupy movement—gets pushed to the back of our historical memory. That movement erupted with such force and in a context that made connections with events in Egypt and events in Tunisia, and then in the fightback of public workers in Wisconsin. So clear—those connections were so clear at that time. And then there were encampments in every major city in this country, and a lot of small cities, too. And all over the world.

As a matter of fact, I personally had the opportunity to spend time at the Occupy site in Philadelphia [*cheers and applause*]—I guess Philadelphia must be in the house—in New York, in Oakland, where we had this amazing, amazing march to shut down the ports. And then Berlin, and London. The Occupy movement contained and still contains so much potential. So I want us to think about the promise of that movement. We cannot assume that simply because the tents are no longer up—although they remain in a few places—doesn't mean the struggle of the 99 percent has been dismantled. Didn't we learn a great deal during that short period of time? The Occupy movement made it possible for us to talk about capitalism in an open, public way, in a way that had not been possible since the 1930s. And so I think we need to celebrate this new possibility and recognize that we still inhabit a political space created by the Occupy movement. We shouldn't take the position that now that the tents are gone nothing is left. There's a great deal left. There's a great deal of activism around evictions especially. Then of course, more recently we witnessed the reelection of Barack Obama. By this time everybody who may have been hoping that Obama was the messiah realized that he was simply the president of the United States of America. Simply the president of the racist, imperialist United States of America. And of course, we're all hoping that things will turn out better during this term, but they won't if we don't stand up and do the work we're required to do.

We learned a lot from that election. It was actually quite incredible. Even more so than the first election. During the first election most people were myopically focused on the individual who was the candidate, right? This time around, many of us were really afraid that the Republican candidate would win, which would mean disaster with respect to political issues. I remember saying to everybody, I am not going to sleep until I hear Romney's concession speech. I remembered in 2000 I went to bed thinking Gore was the new president, but then woke up to an eight-year nightmare. Of course, Romney hadn't even written his concession speech; he had only written a victory speech, so it took a while. But what we learned was that people—young people, Black people, Latinos—people did not allow the voter suppression measures to turn them away. People waited for five and six and seven hours—they sometimes waited in line for seven hours. You might have thought that this was the first election in a free South Africa. Let's not forget the exciting phenomenon that was this past election. It tells us something about our country and what we are capable of achieving.

Now let's talk about the gender gap: many more women voted for Obama than men: 55 to 44. But among Black women 96 percent voted for Obama compared to 87 percent of Black men. Of Latinas, 76 percent compared to 65 percent of Latinos. But as I was saying earlier, what do we do about the fact that a majority of white men voted for Romney? That is scary. It's really scary. It tells us something about the persistence of racism, too. But at the same time we learn that white men no longer have exclusive control over the national agenda. This is a major victory! Incidentally, if you are a white man, you don't necessarily have to identify with that collective "white men" about which I am speaking.

I want now to reiterate a few things that I had said earlier about the campaign on immigrant rights. First of all, let me just say that—and this is a major critique of Obama. I have many critiques of Obama. I think Guantánamo Bay should have been shut down by now. And we should not have gone into Afghanistan. At the same time I try to use a feminist approach that allows me to work the contradiction so that I can be supportive of Obama and I can also be extremely critical of him at the same time.

Among other things, I am critical of the extent to which our political discourse has become so flat. For example, we can't even talk about working-class people anymore. When did everybody become "middle class"? And even those of us who might objectively be "middle class" can still identify with the working class. There's something wrong with the fact that we can not talk about the working class. I was talking about opening up the discursive terrain to be able to talk about capitalism; this means we have to reintroduce the working class into our discourses. Poor people—I mean if you can't talk about the working class, how can you talk about poor people? How can you talk about unemployed people? How can you talk about all of the people who've become a part of surplus populations created by global capitalism and the processes of deindustrialization that first began to happen in the 1980s? So we also have to talk about immigrant rights, because immigrant rights are very much linked to that process of globalization. I think it's good that Obama is planning to push for immigrant rights, but it is about more than the DREAM Act. The DREAM Act is important, but it's a little drop in the bucket. It's hardly a beginning step. And let me say also for those who are opposed to the DREAM Act because it provides pathways to citizenship for people who are in the military—again, you can be opposed to the military and at the same time support the DREAM Act. Just as you can support gay rights within the military and you can say at the same time I want to dismantle the Pentagon.

And also the activism around LGBT issues, and again, not only around marriage equality—I don't know why everything begins to focus around marriage equality. You know, it may be that marriage equality is important as a civil rights issue, but we need to go further than simply applying heteronormative standards to all people who identify as members of the LGBT community. As a matter of fact, what was so exciting about the gay rights movement during its feminist phase, I would say, was its critique of marriage, especially since the institution of marriage was used in an ideologically oppressive way against Black people during slavery, and then later— you remember when Bush argued that what people need is to get married? Poor Black people, all they need to do is get married and suddenly all their problems are going to disappear? When I say critique of marriage, I'm not talking about a critique of relations of intimacy and emotional connections, and the ties that we feel with people with whom we would like to spend our lives. That's not what I'm talking about. I'm talking about the institution as a capitalist institution that's designed to guarantee the distribution of property.

We should also in our activism incorporate strategies to minimize Islamophobia and xenophobia. Defend Muslims who are seriously under attack because of efforts to equate Islam and terrorism. And even people who have little to do with Islam are under attack. Sikhs, for example, who have been killed because their turbans have been misread as Muslim. And as I said before, immigrant rights are so important and it's not just about the DREAM Act and paths to citizenship; it's about welcoming the people who do so much of the labor that fuels the economy: the agricultural labor, the service labor, people who perform the labor that Black people used to perform. This should be considered a part of Black history and a part of the Black freedom struggle.

And then if I had time, I would talk about issues of disability. I'm beyond my time now, so I'll just tell you what I would have talked about had I had more time. I would have said something about food politics and the capitalist production of food that has made so many people ill and has created so much suffering for so many animals. I would have talked about Palestine to a greater extent. And it seems to me that the Black freedom struggle gets extended in many ways in the twenty-first century, and those of us who identify with the struggles of Black people for freedom in the United States of America should clearly identify with our Palestinian sisters and brothers today.

Finally, however we might want to engage in progressive and transformative activism, there is one principle we should remember. This principle is associated with Dr. Martin Luther King and should be the slogan of all of our movements: "Justice is indivisible. Injustice anywhere is a threat to justice everywhere."

TEN

Transnational Solidarities

Speech at Boğaziçi University, Istanbul, Turkey (January 9, 2015)

Hrant Dink remains a potent symbol of the struggle against colonialism, genocide, and racism. Those who assume that it was possible to eradicate his dream of justice, peace, and equality must now know that by striking him down countless Hrant Dinks were created, as people all over the world exclaim, "I am Hrant Dink." We know that his struggle for justice and equality lives on. Ongoing efforts to create a popular intellectual environment within which to explore the contemporary impact of the Armenian genocide are central, I think, to global resistance to racism, genocide, and settler colonialism. The spirit of Hrant Dink lives on and grows stronger and stronger.

I am very pleased that I'm been accorded the opportunity to join a very long list of distinguished speakers who have paid tribute to Hrant Dink. I can say I'm a little intimidated by that prospect as well. I know that those of you who have made it a regular practice to attend these lectures have had the opportunity to hear Arundhati

Roy and Naomi Klein, Noam Chomsky, and Loïc Wacquant. So I hope I live up to your expectations.

Let me also say that I am very pleased that the commemoration of the life and work of Hrant Dink has provided me with an occasion for my very first visit to Turkey. It's hard to believe that it has taken so many decades for me to actually visit this country, since I have dreamed of Istanbul since I was very young, and especially since I learned about the formative influence of Turkish geographies, politics, and intellectual life, and this very university, on a formative influence and close friend, James Baldwin. I can also share with you that as a very young activist—and as I grow older it seems I grow younger as well in my memories and thoughts—I remember reading and feeling inspired by the words of Nâzim Hikmet, as in those days every good communist did. And I can say that when I myself was imprisoned, I was encouraged and emboldened by messages of solidarity and by various descriptions of events organized on my behalf here in Turkey. As I said, I can't believe this is my first trip to Turkey. When I was in graduate school in Frankfurt, my sister made an amazing trip to Turkey, so I'll have to tell her that I finally caught up with her fifty years later.

And since this is my first trip to Turkey, I would like to thank all of those who personally joined the campaign for my freedom in those days, or whose parents were involved, or perhaps whose grandparents were involved in the international movement for my defense. I think far more important than the fact that I was on the FBI's Ten Most Wanted list—which draws applause these days; it tells you what happens if you live long enough, the transformative power of history—is that vast international campaign that achieved what was imagined to be unachievable. That is to say, against all odds we won in our confrontation with the most powerful figures in the US at that time. Let's not forget that Ronald Reagan was the governor of California, Richard Nixon was the president of the US, and J. Edgar Hoover was the head of the FBI.

Often people ask me how I would like to be remembered. My response is that I really am not that concerned about ways in which people might remember me personally. What I do want people to remember is the fact that the movement around the demand for my freedom was victorious. It was a victory against insurmountable odds, even though I was innocent; the assumption was that the power of those forces in the US was so strong that I would either end up in the gas chamber or that I would spend the rest of my life behind bars. Thanks to the movement, I am here with you today.

My relationship with Turkey has been shaped by other movements of solidarity. More recently, I attempted to contribute to the solidarity efforts supporting those who challenged the F-type prisons here in Turkey, including prisoners who joined death fasts. And I've also been active in efforts to generate solidarity around Abdullah Ocalan and other political prisoners, such as Pinar Selek.

Given that my historical relationships with this country have been shaped by circumstances of international solidarity, I have entitled my talk "Transnational Solidarities: Resisting Racism, Genocide, and Settler Colonialism," for the purpose of evoking possible futures, potential circuits connecting movements in various parts of the world, and specifically, in the US, Turkey, and occupied Palestine.

The term "genocide" has usually been reserved for particular conditions defined in accordance with the United Nations Convention on the Prevention and Punishment of the Crime of Genocide, which was adopted on December 9, 1948, in the aftermath of the

fascist scourge during World War II. Some of you are probably familiar with the wording of that convention, but let me share it with
you: "Any of the following acts committed with intent to destroy,
in whole or in part, a national, ethnic, racial, or religious group
as such, killing members of the group, causing serious bodily or
mental harm to members of the group, deliberately inflicting on
the group conditions of life calculated to bring about its physical
destruction in whole or in part, imposing measures intended to
prevent births within the group, and forcibly transferring children
of the group to another group."

This convention was passed in 1948, but it was not rati-
fied by the US until 1987, almost forty years later. However,
just three years after the passage of the convention, a petition
was submitted to the United Nations by the Civil Rights Congress of the US, charging genocide with respect to Black people in the US. This petition was signed by luminaries such as
W. E. B. Du Bois, who at that time was under attack by the government. It was submitted to the UN in New York by Paul Robeson
and it was submitted in Paris by the civil rights attorney William L.
Patterson. Patterson was at that time the head of the Civil Rights
Congress. He was a Black member of the Communist Party, a
prominent attorney who had defended the Scottsboro Nine. His
passport was taken away when he returned. This was during the
era in which communists and those who were accused of being
communists were seriously under attack.

In the introduction to this petition, one can read the following
words: "Out of the inhuman Black ghettos of American cities, out of
the cotton plantations of the South, comes this record of mass slay-
ings on the basis of race, of lives deliberately warped and distorted

by the willful creation of conditions making for premature death, poverty, and disease. It is a record that calls aloud for condemnation, for an end to these terrible injustices that constitute a daily and ever-increasing violation of the United Nations Convention on the Prevention and Punishment of the Crime of Genocide."The introduction continues, "We maintain, therefore, that the oppressed Negro citizens of the United States, segregated, discriminated against, and long the target of violence, suffer from genocide as the result of the consistent, conscious, unified policies of every branch of government."

Then they go on to point out that they will submit evidence proving, in accordance with the convention, the killing of members of the group. They point to police killings—this is 1951—killings by gangs, by the Ku Klux Klan, and other racist groups. They point out that the evidence concerns thousands of people who have been "beaten to death on chain gangs and in the back rooms of sheriffs' offices and in the cells of county jails and precinct police stations and on city streets, who have been framed and murdered by sham legal forms and by a legal bureaucracy. They also point out that a significant number of Black people were killed allegedly for failure to say "sir" to a white person, or to tip their hats, or to move aside.

I mention this historic petition against genocide first because such a charge could have also been launched at the time based on the mass slaughters of Armenians, the death marches, the theft of children and the attempt to assimilate them into dominant culture. I had the opportunity to read the very moving memoir *My Grandmother*, an Armenian Turkish memoir by Fethiye Çetin. I'm certain everyone in this room has read the book. I also learned that as many as two million Turks might have at least one grandparent of Armenian heritage, and that because of prevailing racism, so many people have been prevented from exploring their own family histories.

Reading *My Grandmother*, I thought about the work of a French Marxist anthropologist whose name is Claude Meillassoux. This imposed silence with respect to ancestry reminded me that his definition of slavery has the concept of social death at its core. He defined the slave as subject to a kind of social death—the slave as a person who was not born, *non née*. Of course, there's grave collective psychic damage that is a consequence of not being acknowledged within the context of one's ancestry. Those of us of African descent in the US of my age are familiar with that sense of not being able to trace our ancestry beyond, as in my case, one grandmother. Deprivation of ancestry affects the present and the future. Of course, *My Grandmother* details the process of ethnic cleansing, the death march, the killings by the gendarmes, the fact that when they were crossing a bridge, the grandmother's own grandmother threw two of her grandchildren in the water and made sure they had drowned before she threw herself into the water. And for me the scene so resonated with historical descriptions of slave mothers in the US who killed their children in order to spare them the violence of slavery. Toni Morrison's novel *Beloved*, for which she received the Nobel Prize, is based on one such narrative, the narrative of Margaret Garner.

I also evoke the genocide petition of 1951 because so many of the conditions outlined in that petition continue to exist in the US today. This analysis helps us to understand the extent to which contemporary racist state violence in the US is deeply rooted in genocidal histories, including, of course, the genocidal colonization of indigenous inhabitants of the Americas. A recent book by historian Craig Wilder addresses the extent to which the Ivy League universities, the universities everyone knows all over the world—you mention the name Harvard and that is recognizable virtually everywhere in the world—Harvard, Yale, Princeton, et cetera, were founded on and are deeply implicated in the institution of slavery. But—and in my mind this may be the most important aspect of his research—he discovers that he cannot tell the story of slavery and US higher education without also simultaneously telling the story of the genocidal colonization of Native Americans.

I think it's important to pay attention to the larger methodological implications of such an approach. Our histories never unfold in isolation. We cannot truly tell what we consider to be our own histories without knowing the other stories. And often we discover that those other stories are actually our own stories. This is the admonition "Learn your sisters' stories" by Black feminist sociologist Jacqui Alexander. This is a dialectical process that requires us to constantly retell our stories, to revise them and retell them and relaunch them. We can thus not pretend that we do not know about the conjunctures of race and class and ethnicity and nationality and sexuality and ability.

I cannot prescribe how Turkish people—I've learned in the days since I've been here (actually, this is only my second and a half day here) that it might be better to refer to "people who live in Turkey." I cannot prescribe how you come to grips with the imperial past of this country. But I do know, because I have learned this from Hrant Dink, from Fethiye Çetin, and others, that it has to be possible to speak freely, it has to be possible to engage in free speech. The ethnic-cleansing processes, including the so-called population exchanges at the end of the Ottoman Empire that inflicted incalculable forms of violence on so many populations—Greeks and

Syrians, and, of course, Armenians—have to be acknowledged in the historical record. But popular conversations about these events and about the histories of the Kurdish people in this space have to occur before any real social transformation can be imagined, much less rendered possible.

I tell you that in the United States we are at such a disadvantage because we do not know how to talk about the genocide inflicted on indigenous people. We do not know how to talk about slavery. Otherwise it would not have been assumed that simply because of the election of one Black man to the presidency we would leap forward into a postracial era. We do not acknowledge that we all live on colonized land. And in the meantime, Native Americans live in impoverished conditions on reservations. They have an extremely high incarceration rate—as a matter of fact, per capita the highest incarceration rate—and they suffer disproportionately from such diseases as alcoholism and diabetes. In the meantime, sports teams still mock indigenous people with racially derogatory names, like the Washington Redskins. We do not know how to talk about slavery, except, perhaps, within a framework of victim and victimizer, one that continues to polarize and implicate.

But I can say that, increasingly, young activists are learning how to acknowledge the intersections of these stories, the ways in which these stories are crosshatched and overlaid. Therefore, when we attempt to develop an analysis of the persistence of racist violence, largely directed at young Black men, of which we have been hearing a great deal over this last period, we cannot forget to contextualize this racist violence.

Here in Turkey you are all aware that this past fall and last summer in Ferguson, Missouri, all over the country—in New York, in

Washington, in Chicago, on the West Coast—and, indeed, in other parts of the world, people took to the streets collectively announcing that they absolutely refuse to assent to racist state violence. People took to the streets saying, "No justice, no peace, no racist police." And people have been saying that, contrary to routine police actions and regardless of the collusion of district attorneys with the police, that Black lives do matter. Black lives matter. And we will take to the streets and raise our voices until we can be certain that a change is on the agenda. Social media have been flooded with messages of solidarity from people all over the world in the fall, not only with respect to the failure to indict the police officer who killed Michael Brown in Ferguson, Missouri, but also as a response to the decision of the grand jury in the case of Eric Garner [in New York City]. These demonstrations literally all over the world made it very clear that there is vast potential with respect to the forging of transnational solidarities.

What this means in one sense is that we may be given the opportunity to emerge from the individualism within which we are ensconced in this neoliberal era. Neoliberal ideology drives us to focus on individuals, ourselves, individual victims, individual perpetrators. But how is it possible to solve the massive problem of racist state violence by calling upon individual police officers to bear the burden of that history and to assume that by prosecuting them, by exacting our revenge on them, we would have somehow made progress in eradicating racism? If one imagines these vast expressions of solidarity all over the world as being focused only on the fact that individual police officers were not prosecuted, it makes very little sense. I'm not suggesting that individuals should not be held accountable. Every individual who engages in such a violent act of racism, of terror, should be held accountable. But what I am saying is that we have to embrace projects that address the sociohistorical conditions that enable these acts.

For some time now I have been involved in efforts to abolish the death penalty and imprisonment as the main modes of punishment. I should say that it is not simply out of empathy with the victims of capital punishment and the victims of prison punishment, who are overwhelmingly people of color. It is because these modes of punishment don't work. These forms of punishment do not work when you consider that the majority of people who are in prison are there because society has failed them, because they've had no access to education or jobs or housing or health care. But let me say that criminalization and imprisonment could not solve other problems.

They do not solve the problem of sexual violence either. "Carceral feminism," which is a term that has begun to circulate recently—carceral feminisms, that is to say, feminisms that call for the criminalization and incarceration of those who engage in gender violence—do the work of the state. Carceral feminisms do the work of the state as surely as they focus on state violence and repression as the solution to heteropatriarchy and as the solution, more specifically, to sexual assault. But it does not work for those who are directly involved in the repressive work of the state either. As influenced as many police officers may be by the racism that criminalizes communities of color—and this influence is not limited to white police officers; Black police officers and police officers of color are subject to the same way in which racism structurally defines police work—but even as they may be influenced by this racism, it was not their individual idea to do this. So simply by focusing on the individual as if the individual were an aberration, we inadvertently engage in the process of reproducing the very violence that we assume we are contesting.

How do we move beyond this framework of primarily focusing on individual perpetrators? In the case of Michael Brown in Ferguson, Missouri, we quickly learned about the militarization of the police because of the visual images of their military garb, military vehicles, and military weapons. The militarization of the police in the US, of police forces all over the country has been accomplished in part with the aid of the Israeli government, which has been sharing its training with police forces all over the country since the period in the immediate aftermath of 9/11. As a matter of fact, the St. Louis County Police chief, whose name is Timothy Fitch—and St. Louis, of course, is the setting in which the Ferguson violence took place; Ferguson is a small town in St. Louis County—this chief received "counterterrorism" training in Israel. County sheriffs and police chiefs from all over the country, agents of the FBI, and bomb technicians have been traveling to Israel to get lessons in how to combat terrorism.

The point that I'm making is that while racist police violence, particularly against Black people, has a very long history, going back to the era of slavery, the current context is absolutely decisive. And when one examines the ways in which racism has been further reproduced and complicated by the theories and practices of terrorism and counterterrorism, one begins to perhaps envision the possibility of political alliances that will move us in the direction of transnational solidarities. What was interesting during the protests in Ferguson last summer was that Palestinian activists noticed from the images they saw on social media and on television that tear-gas canisters that were being used in Ferguson were exactly the same tear-gas canisters that were used against them in occupied Palestine. As a matter of fact, a US company, which is called Combined Systems, Incorporated, stamps "CTS" (Combined Tactical Systems) on their tear-gas canisters. When Palestinian activists noticed these canisters in Ferguson, what they did was to tweet advice to Ferguson protesters on how to deal with the tear gas. They suggested, among other things: "Don't keep much distance from the police. If you're close to them, they can't tear gas," because they would be tear-gassing themselves. There was a whole series of really interesting comments for the young activists in Ferguson, who were probably confronting tear gas for the first time in their lives. They didn't necessarily have the experience that some of us older activists have with tear gas.

I'm trying to suggest that there are connections between the militarization of the police in the US, which provides a different context for us to analyze the continuing, ongoing proliferation of racist police violence, and the continuous assault on people in occupied Palestine, the West Bank, and especially in Gaza, given the military violence inflicted on people in Gaza this past summer.

I also want to bring into the conversation one of the most well-known political prisoners in the history of the US. Her name is Assata Shakur. Assata now lives in Cuba, and has lived in Cuba since the 1980s. Not very long ago she was designated as one of the ten most dangerous terrorists in the world. And since it was mentioned that I was on the FBI's Ten Most Wanted list, I would like you to think about what would motivate the decision to place this woman, Assata Shakur, on that list. You can read her history. Her autobiography is absolutely fascinating. She was falsely, fraudulently charged with a whole range of crimes. I won't even mention them. You can read about it in her biography. She was found not guilty on every single charge except the very last one. I wrote a preface to the second edition of her autobiography. Assata, who is actually younger than I am by a few years, is in her late sixties now. She has been leading a productive life in Cuba, studying and teaching and engaging in art. So why would Homeland Security suddenly decide that she is one of the Ten Most Wanted terrorists in the world?

This retroactive criminalization of the late-twentieth-century Black liberation movements through targeting one of the women leaders at that time, who was so systematically pursued, is, I think, an attempt to deter people from engaging in radical political struggle today. This is why I am always so cautious about the use of the term "terrorist." I am cautious, knowing that we have endured a history of unacknowledged terror. As someone who grew up in the most segregated city of the South, my very first memories were of bombs exploding across the street from my family's house simply because a Black person had purchased a house. We actually knew the identities of the Ku Klux Klan people were who were bombing houses and bombing churches. You may be familiar with the bombing of the Sixteenth Street Baptist Church that happened in 1963, when the four young girls, who were all very close to my family, died. But you should know that that was not an unusual occasion. Those bombings happened all the time. Why has that not been acknowledged as an era of terror? So I'm really cautious about the use of that term, because there is almost always a political motivation.

Let me say, as I move toward my conclusion, that I want to be little bit more specific about the importance of feminist theory and analysis. I'm not simply speaking to the women in the audience, because I think feminism provides methodological guidance for all of us who are engaged in serious research and organized activist work. Feminist approaches urge us to develop understandings of social relations, whose connections are often initially only intuited. Everyone is familiar with the slogan "The personal is political"—not only that what we experience on a personal level has profound political implications, but that our interior lives, our emotional lives are very much informed by ideology. We ourselves often do the work of the state in and through our interior lives. What we often assume belongs most intimately to ourselves and to our emotional life has been produced elsewhere and has been recruited to do the work of racism and repression.

Some of us have always insisted on making connections, in terms of prison work, between assaults on women in prison and the larger project of abolishing imprisonment. And this larger project requires us to understand where we figure into transnational solidarity efforts. This means that we have to examine various dimensions of our lives—from social relations, political contexts—but also our interior lives. It's interesting that in this era of global capitalism the corporations have learned how to do that: the corporations have learned how to access aspects of our lives that cause us to often express our innermost dreams in terms of capitalist commodities. So we have internalized exchange value in ways that would have been entirely unimaginable to the authors of *Capital*. But this is the topic of another lecture.

What I want to point out is that the megacorporations have clearly grasped the ways in which what we often consider to be disparate issues are connected. One such corporation, G4S, which is the largest security corporation in the world—and, I evoke G4S because I am certain that they will attempt to take advantage in

France of the current situation in a way that evokes Naomi Klein's analysis of disaster capitalism—G4S, as some of you probably know, has played such an important role in the Israeli occupation of Palestine: running prisons, being involved in checkpoint technology. It's also been involved in the deaths of undocumented immigrants. The case of Jimmy Mubenga is important. He was killed by G4S guards in Britain in the process of being deported to Angola. G4S operates private prisons in South Africa. G4S is the largest corporate employer on the entire continent of Africa. G4S, this megacorporation that is involved in the ownership and operation of prisons, that provides armies with weapons, that provides security for rock stars, also operates centers for abused women and for "young girls at risk." I mention this because it seems that they have grasped the connection in ways that we should have long ago.

Speaking of megacorporations, I heard that students have successfully protested Starbucks. Is today the last day Starbucks will be available on this campus? Hallelujah. Especially since Turkish coffee far exceeds what Starbucks could ever hope for.

My last example is also an example from the US, but it reflects a global pandemic from which no country is exempt. I'm referring to sexual violence, sexual harassment, sexual assault. Intimate violence is not unconnected to state violence. Where do perpetrators of intimate violence learn how to engage in the practices of violence? Who teaches them that violence is okay? But this is, of course, another question. I do want to evoke the case of a young woman by the name of Marissa Alexander. You know the names of Michael Brown and Eric Garner. Add the name of Marissa Alexander to that list, a young Black woman who felt compelled to go to extremes to prevent her abusive husband from attacking her. She fired a weapon in the air. No one was hit. But in the very same judicial district where Trayvon Martin—you remember his name—was killed, and where George Zimmerman, his killer, was acquitted, Marissa Alexander was sentenced to twenty years for trying to defend herself against sexual assault. Recently she faced a possible resentencing to sixty years, and therefore she engaged in a plea bargain, which means that she will be wearing an electronic bracelet for the next period.

Racist and sexual violence are practices that are not only tolerated but explicitly—or if not explicitly, then implicitly—encouraged. When these modes of violence are recognized—and they are often hidden and rendered invisible—they are most often the most dramatic examples of structural exclusion and discrimination. I think it would be important to go further developing that analysis, but I am going to conclude by saying that the greatest challenge facing us as we attempt to forge international solidarities and connections across national borders is an understanding of what feminists often call "intersectionality." Not so much intersectionality of identities, but intersectionality of struggles.

Let us not forget the impact of Tahrir Square and the Occupy movement all over the world. And since we are gathered here in Istanbul, let us not forget the Taksim Gezi Park protesters. Oftentimes people argue that in these more recent movements there were no leaders, there was no manifesto, no agenda, no demands, so therefore the movements failed. But I'd like to point out that Stuart Hall, who died just a little over a year ago, urged us to distinguish between outcome and impact. There is a difference between outcome and impact. Many people assume that because the encampments are gone and nothing tangible was produced, that there was no outcome. But when we think about the impact of these imaginative and innovative actions and these moments where people learned how to be together without the scaffolding of the state, when they learned to solve problems without succumbing to the impulse of calling the police, that should serve as a true inspiration for the work that we will do in the future to build these transnational solidarities. Don't we want to be able to imagine the expansion of freedom and justice in the world, as Hrant Dink urged us to do—in Turkey, in Palestine, in South Africa, in Germany, in Colombia, in Brazil, in the Philippines, in the US?

If this is the case, we will have to do something quite extraordinary: We will have to go to great lengths. We cannot go on as usual. We cannot pivot the center. We cannot be moderate. We will have to be willing to stand up and say no with our combined spirits, our collective intellects, and our many bodies.

Index

"Passim" (literally "scattered") indicates intermittent discussion of a topic over a cluster of pages.

About Haymarket Books

Haymarket Books is a nonprofit, progressive book distributor and publisher, a project of the Center for Economic Research and Social Change. We believe that activists need to take ideas, history, and politics into the many struggles for social justice today. Learning the lessons of past victories, as well as defeats, can arm a new generation of fighters for a better world. As Karl Marx said, "The philosophers have merely interpreted the world; the point, however, is to change it."

We take inspiration and courage from our namesakes, the Haymarket Martyrs, who gave their lives fighting for a better world. Their 1886 struggle for the eight-hour day reminds workers around the world that ordinary people can organize and struggle for their own liberation.

For more information and to shop our complete catalog of titles, visit us online at www.haymarketbooks.org.

Also available from Haymarket Books

AFRICAN STRUGGLES TODAY:
SOCIAL MOVEMENTS SINCE INDEPENDENCE
Peter Dwyer and Leo Zeilig

THE BLACK PANTHERS SPEAK
Edited by Philip S. Foner, foreword by Barbara Ransby

THE BLACK POWER MIXTAPE: 1967–1975
Göran Hugo Olssen

BOOTS RILEY: TELL HOMELAND SECURITY—WE ARE THE BOMB
Boots Riley, foreword by Adam Mansbach

BOYCOTT, DIVESTMENT, SANCTIONS: THE GLOBAL STRUGGLE FOR PALESTINIAN RIGHTS
Omar Barghouti

CAPITALISM: A GHOST STORY
Arundhati Roy

FROM #BLACKLIVESMATTER TO BLACK LIBERATION
Keeanga-Yamahtta Taylor

About the Authors

Angela Y. Davis is a political activist, scholar, author, and speaker. She is an outspoken advocate for the oppressed and exploited, writing on Black liberation, women's liberation, prison abolition, and international solidarity with Palestine. She is the author of several books, including *Women, Race, and Class* and *Are Prisons Obsolete?* She is the subject of the acclaimed documentary *Free Angela and All Political Prisoners* and is professor emerita at the University of California, Santa Cruz.

Frank Barat is a human rights activist and author. He was the coordinator of the Russell Tribunal on Palestine and is now the president of the Palestine Legal Action Network. His books include *Gaza in Crisis*, *Corporate Complicity in Israel's Occupation*, and *On Palestine*.

One of America's most provocative public intellectuals, Cornel West has been a champion for racial justice since childhood. His writing, speaking, and teaching weave together the traditions of the black Baptist Church, progressive politics, and jazz. The *New York Times* has praised his "ferocious moral vision." His many books include *Race Matters*, *Democracy Matters*, and his autobiography, *Brother West: Living and Loving Out Loud*.